planting *trust,*
knowing peace

Secrets of Soul Gardening Series

Tilling the Soul: Prayer Penetrates Your Pain

Cultivating a Forgiving Heart: Forgiveness Frees You to Flourish

Weathering the Storms: Fear Fades as Your Faith Deepens

Planting Trust, Knowing Peace: Trust Grows as You Embrace the Father's Love

secrets of soul gardening

trust grows as you embrace the Father's love

planting *trust,*
knowing peace

denise george

GRAND RAPIDS, MICHIGAN 49530 USA

Planting Trust, Knowing Peace
Copyright © 2005 by Denise George

Requests for information should be addressed to:

Zondervan, *Grand Rapids, Michigan 49530*

Library of Congress Cataloging-in-Publication Data

George, Denise.
    Planting trust, knowing peace : trust grows as you embrace the Father's love / Denise George.
        p. cm. — (Secrets of soul gardening)
    Summary: "An in-depth six-week devotional Bible study for women in the Secrets of Soul
Gardening series. This volume focuses on the importance of trusting God as your perfect and loving
father"—Provided by publisher.
    Includes bibliographical references and index.
    ISBN-10: 0-310-25119-2
    ISBN-13: 978-0-310-25119-4
    1. Trust in God—Christianity. 2. Peace of mind—Religious aspects—Christianity. 3. Christian
women—Prayer-books and devotions—English. 4. Christian women—Religious life. I. Title.
    BV4637.G47 2005
    242'.643—dc22

            2005005947

Published in association with the literary agency of Alive Communications, Inc., 7680 Goddard Street, Suite 200, Colorado Springs, CO 80920.

Interior design by Ruth Bandstra

Composition by Beth Shagene

Printed in the United States of America

05 06 07 08 09 10 11 12 /❖ DCI/ 15 14 13 12 11 10 9 8 7 6 5 4 3 2 1

For the Reverend Roger Salter and Mrs. Maurreen Salter

Spiritual mentors
and
good friends

Contents

Forewords by Sheila and Cokiesha Bailey

In your dream of dreams, if you could be made over, what would you look like? What features of your human frame would be enlarged or diminished, reconstructed or removed? Perhaps you enjoy, as I do, watching the extreme makeover shows on television and seeing a team of medical specialists, cosmetology experts, and professional trainers bring tears of joy to individuals as their dreams of physical beauty become reality.

Similarly, Denise George comes into your life through the pages of this book with a team of biblical and contemporary personalities designed to achieve an *interior* makeover. "Anyone who belongs to Christ is a new person. The past is forgotten, and everything is new" (2 Cor. 5:17 CEV). No longer must you be haunted by fears and failures nor limited by accomplishments and attainments. Your beauty will exude from the inside-out as you appropriate biblical principles into your daily life. As the J. B. Phillips paraphrase of Romans 12:2 states, "Don't let the world around you squeeze you into its mold; but let God remold your minds from within." In other words, experience the makeover of "interiority" through the renewing power of the living Christ.

Whether your relationships with your earthly father and heavenly Father to this point have been fertile or rocky, you can be a person planted and nurtured by the Divine Gardener, bearing the fruit of the Spirit. You can be different and you can make a difference. Hugh of St. Victor (1096–1141) expresses the results of such an interior makeover: "Suddenly I feel myself transformed and changed. It is joy unspeakable. My mind is exhilarated; I lose the memory of past trials; my intelligence is clarified; my desires are satisfied. I grasp something inwardly as with the embracement of love."

SHEILA M. BAILEY (MOTHER)
PRESIDENT, E. K. BAILEY MINISTRIES, DALLAS, TEXAS

No father-daughter relationship is perfect. I shared a special relationship with my father and so did my siblings, but because we all have human limitations there were areas where we had to rely on God as our Supreme Father, times when each of us had to crawl up into his lap to be held and reassured. We had to remember that although we adored our earthly father, our heavenly Father was the only "dad" with a perfect character. He is and will be the only one who can "meet all of our needs according to his riches in heaven." By getting to know God's qualities, we gained new perspective and a better way of loving, forgiving, and receiving love from our earthly father.

In this heartfelt book, Denise George takes our hand and leads us into a fresh way of living and learning from our experiences. She celebrates what a godly father looks like and allows us to feel the pain of relationships where fathers may have been present, but emotionally absent. She helps us to understand that suffering can come in the form of a damaged relationship with one's father, but even then, God continues to work things out for our good. As Mrs. Charles Spurgeon, wife of the famous preacher, once said, "God uses suffering so that our hearts will be purified and so that he may be glorified." Denise echoes that hope-filled sentiment. She allows us to feel God's welcoming arms and to hear his soft voice whispering how much he loves us.

I like to think of Denise as a C.S.D.L., a "certified spiritual diver and lifeguard." She recognizes that many women have packed up their secret pain and thrown it overboard into the sea of life, hoping to never see it again. She understands that some have even given up on their broken relationships with their fathers and are living a lifeless life doing the "dead man's float." Denise plunges into these choppy, uncharted waters and helps us to regain emotional "consciousness" through the Word of God. She brings up the stuff that we hoped would never be recovered and reassures us that we will survive the emotional waves as we unpack the hurt. She lovingly aids us as we unlock what we thought was unwanted trash, only to discover rich and rare treasures. By God's grace, we learn how to breathe again.

COKIESHA L. BAILEY (DAUGHTER)
CHRISTIAN SPEAKER/AUTHOR, BIRMINGHAM, ALABAMA

Acknowledgments

My heartfelt thanks to my wonderful editor, Cindy Hays Lambert. This is our fourth book together in the Secrets of Soul Gardening series. Thank you, Cindy, for laboring closely with me in this joint effort to reach out in Christ's name to hurting women. You've become a dear friend. Thanks too to the rest of the team in Grand Rapids. I am pleased to call Zondervan my publisher.

My gratitude to my husband, Dr. Timothy George, and to my grown children: Alyce, Christian, and his bride of one year, Rebecca. A special thank you to the many people, colleagues, and friends who encouraged me and prayed for me during the writing of this book. I appreciate you so much! I also wish to thank the many women who shared with me their personal stories. And I want to extend a special note of appreciation to Dr. and Mrs. Jerry (Pat) Batson of Beeson Divinity School for opening your beautiful Florida home and allowing me quiet time alone to pray, think, and write. You gave me a priceless gift!

There is a time for everything, and a season for every activity under heaven:

A time to be born and a time to die,

A time to plant and a time to uproot,

A time to kill and a time to heal,

A time to tear down and a time to build,

A time to weep and a time to laugh,

A time to mourn and a time to dance,

A time to scatter stones and a time to gather them,

A time to embrace and a time to refrain,

A time to search and a time to give up,

A time to keep and a time to throw away,

A time to tear and a time to mend,

A time to be silent and a time to speak,

A time to love and a time to hate,

A time for war and *a time for peace*.

Ecclesiastes 3:1–8

Before You Begin

I learned to trust in a garden. As a child, I was blessed with kind and loving caretakers—my parents, my grandparents, and an interesting assortment of aunts, uncles, and family friends—who provided safe, well-tended ground in which my five little cousins and I could grow up straight and strong and sprout healthy leaves.

On their small farm in northern Georgia, "Mama" and "Papa" (my maternal grandparents) gave each grandchild a biblical foundation and a "theological education." Like six baby ducklings, we grandkids waddled behind Papa as he walked through his hand-tilled vegetable gardens. He taught. We admired and listened. With great patience, Papa showed us how to prepare soil and plant seedlings. We watched with awe as each tiny sprout raised higher its tender head and turned our ground a glorious green. We helped Papa fertilize the plants with smelly, but soil-enriching "gifts," generously supplied by his pony, Inky. We worked hard together, clearing new fields and weeding out wild growth.

Papa gave us complete freedom to run and play inside the fenced yard and garden that encircled their white gabled home. But he strictly marked the boundary that surrounded the patch of poison ivy. He pointed to the patch of shiny leaves and told us firmly: "Leaves of three, let 'em be." When we forgot and overstepped our boundaries, we experienced the painful results. We couldn't hide our forgetfulness for long. It paraded itself on our arms and legs in an itchy tattletale rash.

The poison ivy patch grew and spread and soon became such a problem that Papa decided to pull it up and burn it. One afternoon, armed with gloves, long sleeves, thick socks, and tall boots, Papa destroyed the poisonous patch of plants. Jerked it up clear down to the roots. And he made sure it never grew there again.

Several days later, as Papa sat in the porch swing and gazed upon the strip of newly bared ground, he had an idea. "Why don't we plant something useful in that empty patch?" he suggested. I immediately saw the twinkle in Mama's eyes. "When I was a little girl," she said, "my grandmother grew herbs. She'd make some into a tea that settled our upset stomachs. And she'd make some into a paste and rub it on our bug bites. Her herbs would cure most any ailment."

Mama's vivid memories ignited our interest. So the next morning we piled into Papa's big, black Buick and headed to the farmer's market in downtown Rossville. We bought little pots of parsley, cilantro, dill, marjoram, peppermint, sage, oregano, chamomile, lavender, and basil. By that afternoon, we had planted a good-sized herb garden. As we sat on the ground with dirty bare feet and sweaty brows, and admired our labor, we gently pressed the leaves and smelled our fingers. We discovered each herb had its own special fragrance. That evening Mama snipped some sprigs of parsley and cilantro, and stirred them into her soup. She also clipped a cluster of chamomile and made a warm tea. We grandkids visited the local library, checked out books on old-time herbs, looked at the pictures, and listened eagerly as Mama and Papa revealed to us their magical herbal secrets.

Almost a half century later, I continue to grow a garden of herbs in my backyard. I still eagerly study their remarkable secrets. And I continue to marvel at their ancient medicinal properties. Whenever I burn my hand, I instinctively reach for a broken stem of aloe vera, and dab its healing gel on my skin—just like my grandmother did, and her grandmother did, and her grandmother did, and Egyptian grandmothers did back in 1500 BC. And when I feel my throat getting scratchy, and know a cold is coming on, I still turn to the miraculous immune system-booster herb *cinnamomum* (cinnamon) that God gave the sore-throated children of Israel during their trek through an unhealthy wilderness.

Not until many years later—after my grandparents' deaths, after weeds overwhelmed those bountiful gardens of my childhood, after I married and moved far away—did I understand and appreciate the simple theology of that childhood herb garden. My grandparents had taught me a valuable lesson when they uprooted poison ivy and replanted healing herbs, and it's one that works just as well in our lives as in our gardens. God the Father yearns for his daughters to realize that we do not have to live a lifetime influenced and dictated by past hurts. We can choose to uproot past pain, to destroy its poisonous influence over our adult lives, and plant in its place seeds that will produce fruits of healing and peace.

Planting Trust, Knowing Peace

During a Thanksgiving dinner many years ago, my then five-year-old son, Christian, sat at the food-laden table eyeing my dad, his grandfather. Daddy was a tall, strong man with a deep voice. Christian watched him closely as Daddy skillfully carved the giant turkey. Then Christian turned to me and, with eyes wide, he whispered: "Mommy, is Granddaddy *God?*"

"No, son," I said and smiled. "Granddaddy's not God, but he's real close!"

I had a father—for fifty years—who was kind and gentle and loving, and who taught me much about my heavenly Father. Blessed is the girl whose father gives her affection, kindness, understanding, protection, loving discipline, and provision. He demonstrates to her the beautiful qualities of her heavenly Father. Perhaps you had a father like this.

But perhaps you didn't. You may be one of the many women today hurting because they did not have fathers who loved, nurtured, and showed them the qualities of their heavenly Father. Some women didn't have a father involved in their lives at all. They might have never even met or known their father. Others spend their adult years seriously suffering—physically, emotionally, mentally, and spiritually—because of unloving, uncaring, undependable earthly fathers.[1] Personalities and actions of fathers can range from violently abusive to incredibly loving. Most fathers probably fall somewhere between these two extremes—decent men but subject to human error and human ways.

I once befriended a woman who had been hurt deeply in her childhood by her father. Marla still suffered from the memories of his abuse. That pain had left her with little capacity to trust, making it impossible for her to make and keep friends. She lost several jobs because of her inability to work well with colleagues. Her personal suffering also affected her husband and children. Though her husband was kind, she often lashed out at him for no apparent reason. She disciplined her children too harshly. Though her abuse was long past, it exerted a powerful influence on her present.

Perhaps the most devastating effect of her father's abuse was how it horribly distorted her view of God. She couldn't imagine that her heavenly Father could be loving and nurturing. That's what a little girl does. She looks at her earthly father to learn about her heavenly Father. Whether for good or bad, human dads paint a portrait of the heavenly Father. And unless intervention and transformation happen, inept earthly fathers—like Marla's dad—influence a girl's life, faith, family, and future for as long as she lives.

Marla craved the loving, intimate relationship with God that I, and other Christian women, enjoyed. But, for a long time, Marla couldn't find that peace and joy. Only through intensive Scripture-study, prayer, counseling, and Christian friends, did Marla come to understand that God, her heavenly Father, was nothing like her human father. As she studied the attributes of God, Marla began to see a true picture of him. She dipped her brushes into the paint of Scripture, and created a more accurate portrait of her heavenly Father. And God transformed her heart, her mind, her thoughts, and her life. Marla learned that "Jesus Christ came to set us free—free from the consequences of sin and death, *but also free from the crippling patterns and experiences of the past.*"[2]

Jesus called his heavenly Father "Abba." Translated, "Abba" means "Daddy," suggesting an intimate, close relationship between father and child. Jesus shows us that his Father—God—is also our Father. Jesus instructed his disciples to pray "our Father" in Matthew 6:9–13. We too, as daughters of God the Father, can reach up to God with the endearing words "Abba—Daddy." Jesus' own relationship to his heavenly Father is our model. He depended on his Father because he trusted his Father.

The Garden of Your Heart

How about you? How deeply do you trust God? How did your own positive and negative experiences shape your portrait of your heavenly Father? Throughout these pages you will meet women who have grown up with godly and ungodly fathers. I hope that within these stories, you can find your own story, or the story of someone you know and/or love.

You and I are about to begin a six-week journey together. During the first three weeks, we will dig into childhood events that shaped your view of fatherhood. We'll explore your early experiences with your father—the good, the bad, and the ugly. We will deal with them—keeping the good, throwing away the bad, and uprooting the pain. During the final three weeks, we will focus on your eternal and forever Father—your Father in heaven—the one who waits for you to fall into his loving arms and welcomes you into his family. He is your ultimate Father. You are his beloved daughter, whom he loves unconditionally. As you allow him to refather you and as you "plant" your trust completely in him, he will transform the garden of your heart into one filled with his hope, joy, and peace.

How to Use This Book

Each week of *Planting Trust, Knowing Peace* is divided into five daily readings. Each day you are invited to take time to bask in "Daily Sunlight." This daily devotional experience is for your personal interaction with God, to work through in solitude and prayer. As sunshine is essential to the growth of a plant, I pray "Daily Sunlight" will help you grow deeper spiritual roots in God's Word. [Note: If you did not know your father, or if he died when you were very young, you may want to substitute a man who was a father figure to you. He might be a grandfather, stepfather, older brother, uncle, pastor, Sunday school teacher, etc.]

A group Bible study, "Your Weekly Feeding," follows every five days of personal "Daily Sunlight." Just like all plants need to be fed rich nourishing food, Christian women must also feed regularly on God's rich and nourishing Word. This section has been written so that you might grow in God's Word together with other women in a group setting (no additional preparation is required for this meeting). If you are not already involved with a weekly Bible study group, I encourage you to get together with a few friends, neighbors, or fellow church members, and work through the six "Your Weekly Feeding" sections.

Now, let us begin our journey.

Your Human Father

Week 1: A Time to Keep

Day 1: The teaching father

> Children should be taught about God in a simple, loving way so they can learn to trust Him and begin to know Him as a kind and loving Father who made them, not perfectly but with all they need to grow in His love.
>
> Joseph F. Girzone, *Never Alone*

During this first week, I want to introduce you to some extraordinary dads. The first one is Dr. E. K. Bailey, a well-known pastor, and father of Cokiesha, a young woman enrolled in Beeson Divinity School at Samford University in Birmingham, Alabama.

"Many people admired my father because of his preaching abilities," Cokiesha told me. "His peers referred to him as, 'a preacher's preacher.' Some were inspired by him because he was a visionary who was committed to creating new ways and methods of ministering God's never-changing Word. Others marveled at his commitment to train and encourage hundreds of young ministers and their families each year. His mentors were pleased that he had become one of America's sought-after expository preachers and influential international leaders."

Yet, Cokiesha remembers him in a special way. "When I reflect upon the things that I admired the most about my father, it was not the time he spent training, teaching, preaching, or 'pastoring,' but the time he spent 'shepherding' our home. He was truly a hero at home. I thank God for his natural, God-given gifts and talents. But I am most grateful that he was a man who balanced his time in such a way that our family (my mother Sheila, my sister, Shenikwa, my brother, Emon, and I) felt as though we were just as valuable as his staff members, friends, sons in the ministry, church members, and book projects."

Cokiesha remembers her dad as a teaching father. He taught her practical life-lessons that remain deeply embedded in her heart and mind. Some of those lessons were:

(About work and work ethics): "Work hard! When you become discouraged and begin to second-guess yourself, pray and ask God to strengthen you and to guard your mind. Get some rest and then work harder. If you're working on a project and things go sour, pray, get some rest and start over if you have to. Remember, a well-rested body and mind is just as important as a prepared message. Be on time. Leave the house early enough to get to work on time. If you leave early, you will not be late, even if there are unexpected setbacks or delays in traffic. Get to work twenty to thirty minutes early if you can, get coffee if you need to, spend some time in prayer, organize your work area, and start working on time. As you are working, pray that God will allow you to produce quality work. Work with a spirit of excellence and allow your work to be a means of worship unto the Lord. Be a person who uses creativity, is committed to encouraging others, and is an effective communicator. Set spiritual, professional, and personal goals, and hold yourself accountable."

(About education): "Always study and stay fresh in your thoughts and ideas."

(About men): "Always encourage them and make them feel as though you cherish their thoughts and opinions. After you have asked a man a question, wait patiently for his response. Men think slower than women. Try not to interrupt him when he is talking. Women's brains move so much faster, after you ask him the question, wait for him to respond and conclude. My dad believed that men were visual and women were emotional. 'Men like for women to look good and smell good.' He was so happy to get home at the end of the day and my mom would have on something pretty, and she would have the house smelling so good because she had cooked his favorites, and was wearing one of his favorite fragrances. I always saw him light up if things were neat and if Mama looked like 'a million bucks.' He believed that it was easier for a woman to fall for a guy based on his personality, but that men normally fall for what they see first, then they became interested in the personality. He encouraged us to always look our best and to be intentional about how we present ourselves in the way we look, the way we behave, and the way we treat others."

(About money): "'Don't act big when little gotchya!' That was one of Dad's favorite things to say to us when our taste in food and clothes exceeded our budget. He insisted that we live within our means and resist the temptation to overspend. He believed if we would tithe our money, and be faithful over the things that God blessed us with, that God would bless us 'exceeding, abundantly, above all that we could ask or think.'"

(About pain and tragedy): "'God uses the spade of sorrow to dig the well of joy.' Daddy believed that everyone had to endure sorrowful times because, during those seasons, God shows us how to trust him more. He taught me that 'joy is always on the other side of sorrow.' He said that 'No one can drink grapes, they must first be crushed. God must hurt us deeply in order to use us significantly.' That phrase is one of the things that my dad said constantly, and I hear those words ringing in my ears even to this day. I see now, through his suffering, and the suffering of other family members, how God encourages us to be more like Jesus. I see how many facets of [Christ's] character we'd never see if we didn't suffer, and how he uses those experiences to get more glory, and to give us a greater testimony. Because of my own suffering and my father's teachings, I see how God takes our 'lemons and makes lemonade.' After suffering, I see how God lifts up our heads and replenishes our joy. He refreshes our spirits, and he uses us to be greater witnesses for him."

(About integrity, trust, and dependability): "He believed that we should be men and women of our word. That when we tell people we are going to do something, we should be sure to follow through. Keeping our word is honorable, and we should live lives of integrity. He thought our names should be synonymous with 'follow-up.' He believed it was not enough to have good intentions, but to have a reputation of having good follow-through, and bringing to closure the things we began. With that, if people are accustomed to us being a man or woman of our word, we can tell them something as silly as, 'A mouse can pull a house,' and they ought to be so confident in our ability to come through, they'll just 'hitch him up.'"

(About loving others): "'Love people and forgive them.' Growing up in a pastor's home was a wonderful experience. There were lots of rewards and some challenges. Sometimes there were even disappointments because people expected you to be upright, forgiving, loving, loyal, and honest even when they were not. My dad encouraged us to always 'take the high road,' meaning that the 'low road' was 'getting back' at people. He said 'God will take care of people when they have wronged us, and to never try to get back at people.' He said that we should 'pray for people, forgive them, and continue to love them, just as Jesus would.'"

(About laughter): "'Laugh regularly and make new mistakes.' Daddy had a hearty laugh, and he passed one down to me. I love laughing; it makes me feel like life has no worries. Furthermore, it's contagious. Daddy suggested that we 'always find time to have fun and laugh with others.' He was a stickler when it came to doing a good job in church, at home, and in the work world. He believed that 'it is natural for people to make mistakes,' but he believed that when people were told that 'something can be done a better way, they should try those ways.' He said, 'people shouldn't keep making the same mistake over and over again. When you make a mistake, it should be a *new* one.'"

(About ministry): "He'd say, 'We can't take an eight-track church into a CD world.' I loved that statement because we believe God's *message* should not change, but the *method* should change in order to minister to upcoming generations."

(About personal faith): "'A person's life rises and falls around his or her devotional life.' Daddy believed our prayer and devotional life 'should be consistent,' and that 'our relationship with God will sustain us during life's difficult moments.'

"My dad experienced many physical setbacks including diabetes, kidney cancer, nasal cancers, and lung cancer," Cokiesha remembers. "He believed many of his battles could have been prevented by eating healthier and exercising more. He urged my family to 'take care of God's temples' and to 'eat well and exercise regularly.'"

Before Cokiesha left home and entered seminary, her father told her: "Just be the best Cokiesha Bailey that you can be, work hard, be disciplined, and God will honor that. Use what you have and start where you are." "Before I hugged him," Cokiesha remembers, "I felt my eyes filling up with tears, and he said to me: 'One day people are going to look at you and say, "That's E. K. Bailey's daughter."' Then he sat back with a heart of satisfaction and told me to go and make him proud."

A few days before Dr. Bailey died, Cokiesha wanted to stay at her father's side instead of returning to her seminary classes. "I was so used to him advising me that I had become dependent upon his wisdom. I waited for him to say, 'Well, you can stay with me for a few more days just in case something happens.' Instead he looked at me and said: 'I can't swim for you any longer, Cokiesha. I have taught you how to swim. Now just do it.'"

Cokiesha remembers how his words made her feel. "I felt so relieved that he trusted me. But it broke my heart because I didn't want to make that decision. I wanted him to make it for me. Now, months after his death, I think of that moment, and I smile because he must have felt great satisfaction knowing that he did the best he could as a parent, and now he could die in peace knowing his family was trained and equipped for the rest of the journey without him. I praise God for that moment and for his precious response."

Cokiesha concludes: "I am a better woman because the Lord allowed me to be taught, mentored, and influenced by a loving, compassionate, caring, and considerate father and mother. I am indebted to them for their sacrificial love, encouragement, and confidence. I feel celebrated as a young Christian woman because they rooted for my future. And most of all, because they introduced me to the greatest gift I have ever known—Jesus Christ."

Daily Sunlight

Your Personal Time to Grow:

Read 1 John 4:13–16. What do these verses say to you about God's love and about the role of Jesus and the Holy Spirit in your life?

_____

_____

_____

_____

_____

No father is perfect, of course, but in what ways did Cokiesha's father prove to be a good parent? A loving dad? A teaching father? How did Cokiesha's father compare with your dad?

_____

_____

_____

_____

What godly attributes did Dr. Bailey instill within his daughter? What godly attributes did your father instill within you?

_____

_____

_____

_____

_____

What are those things Cokiesha needs to keep near to her heart from her dad's influence and teachings? What are those things that you keep near to your heart from your relationship with your dad?

_____

_____

_____

_____

_____

Your Personal Prayer:

Father, a kind and responsible earthly dad is a precious gift from you. Help me to remember that no dad is perfect, and that all human beings make mistakes. Show me how to thank and bless my dad for the good he gave me, and to forgive him for any pain he caused me. In Jesus' name, amen.

Day 2: The sacrificing father

> A daughter needs a dad who will make sacrifices so she will not have to sacrifice.
>
> Gregory E. Lang, *Why a Daughter Needs a Dad*

D aughter." It's a beautiful word that denotes love, care, and deep devotion. When spoken from a dedicated father's mouth—like Cokiesha Bailey's dad, the word takes on an even more special meaning. A strong connection seals the relational bond between a loving father and his daughter. A woman who has known the gift of a dependable and devoted Christian dad will step into the future with confidence and excitement. Her life has been rooted and nurtured by a spiritually supportive father, and she can bravely rise up to face life's many challenges and inevitable storms.

Cokiesha is fortunate. She had a wise, teaching father, one who loved her and prepared her for a life of love and ministry. Every girl, every woman, yearns to be loved like this—unconditionally—by one of the most significant people in her life—her father. She wants to trust him completely. She wants his total acceptance and approval. She wants to be important to him, to be valued, and to be included in his life. She wants to be protected, and to feel physically and emotionally safe. She wants a father who kindly meets her needs—physical, spiritual, emotional, and intellectual. She wants to be listened to, to be understood and respected, to be taken seriously as a significant person in her own right. She craves a loving touch, a hug, a pat on the back. She desires affirmation and praise. She wants to be taught life's lessons; to be encouraged; to be guided by a wise, caring hand; and to be disciplined with gentleness and grace. She yearns for the comfort of a dad's dependability and consistency, to know that he will always be there for her. She wants a father who will allow her to take a risk, to teach her how to "swim on her own," and comfort her if she fails. Every girl, every woman, yearns for a loving father who will give her both roots (as a child) and wings (as an adult). Cokiesha's father gave her all these things. He equipped her well for life and ministry.

This type of devoted father makes a tremendous difference in the life of a woman. Girls who have good fathers tend to do better in adult life than girls who don't. More and more research is showing that a woman's self-esteem, self-confidence, marriage, parenting, and well-being are all deeply rooted in her early father-daughter relationship—especially during those first seven crucial years of her childhood. A devoted dad will influence a woman for good in every aspect of her future life.

What makes a good father? A dad who deeply loves his daughter. A dad who will sacrifice his ambition and pride to be a good parent. A dad who invites a daughter's undivided trust. Such a dad was Jairus. Jairus was a Pharisee, a high-ranking member of the Jewish religious party.[1] He held an important and prestigious position at the synagogue in Capernaum. Like other Pharisees in leadership, Jairus had an authoritative presence about him. He was well-respected. The Pharisees, however, had little respect for Jesus. They constantly tested him and degraded him. They considered him a false teacher, a blasphemer, and a Jew who didn't observe their man-made laws and daily observances.

When Jairus's twelve-year-old daughter became seriously ill, his important position and fine clothes meant little to him. Jesus had just crossed the lake by boat, and had docked in Capernaum. Shoving his way through a large crowd of people, Jairus threw himself down at Jesus' feet, and began to beg Jesus to come to his home and heal his sick daughter.

Gone was his arrogance and pride as he pleaded with Jesus for help. His dignity dashed, his fine clothes drenched in sweat and dust, his head bowed low, Jairus cried out for all to hear: "My little daughter is dying. Please come and put your hands on her so that she will be healed and live" (Mark 5:23).

No doubt, the crowd of common folk gasped at such a sight. The mighty leader lay in the dirt at the feet of the ragtag preacher, the one who had been rumored to heal the sick. Why did Jairus choose to swallow his pride and humiliate himself before Jesus? Jairus loved his daughter. No price proved too high to save his little girl's life. If even a remote chance existed that Jesus could actually heal his daughter, Jairus would throw his self-respect to the wind and, in front of all his colleagues, beg Jesus for help.

Jesus saw Jairus's love and faith, and he went with him. On the way to Jairus's house, Jesus stopped to heal a bleeding woman. During his conversation with the woman, some men came from Jairus's house and told him: "Your daughter is dead." And they added: "Why bother the teacher any more?" Jesus calmly looked into Jairus's saddened eyes, and told him: "Don't be afraid; just believe" (v. 36).

When Jesus arrived at Jairus's home, the crying and loud wailing had already begun. Jesus took Jairus and his wife, as well as Peter, James, and John, into the child's room. Then Jesus took the dead girl's hand and told her to get up. Immediately, the girl stood up and walked around. The sacrifice of a loving father, Jairus, had saved his daughter's life.

Surely, every daughter needs a dad like Jairus. He loved his twelve-year-old girl so much, he gave up his self-respect and community prestige to rescue her from death.

Daily Sunlight

Your Personal Time to Grow:

Read Mark 5:21–24, 35–43. How did Jairus prove to be a good dad to his daughter?

_____

_____

_____

_____

If you could speak with Jairus's daughter, what would you ask her? What could she teach you?

_____

_____

_____

_____

Has your father ever sacrificed for you? In what way? If your answer is yes, what difference did it make in your life?

_____

_____

_____

_____

_____

What are the things in your relationship with your father that you want to keep always and remember?

_____

_____

_____

_____

_____

Your Personal Prayer:

Dear God, I pray that throughout the pages of this book, you will help me to come to grips with my childhood. Show me what caused so much of my pain — the hurt still present in my life. Teach me to understand my present suffering and how it came to be. In your Son's name, amen.

Day 3: The caring father

> "Daughter, your faith has healed you. Go in peace and be freed from your suffering."
>
> Jesus in Mark 5:34

On the way to Jairus's house, Jesus stopped to heal a bleeding woman. (You can read her story in Mark 5:25–34.) Who was this woman? Was she an important enough person that Jesus should pause to help her when an important synagogue leader's daughter lay dying?

No, she wasn't an important person to society. She was a "common" woman. Mark doesn't even mention her name. She had no status. She held no high position. She had no money. Not only was she a "nobody" according to society, she was also an "untouchable." She was hurting and sick and bleeding. In fact, she had been bleeding uncontrollably for twelve years—the same number of years that Jairus's daughter had been alive. She had spent all her money on doctors who had offered her cureless "cures." Her condition grew worse with every passing day.

In that day, a bleeding woman was an unclean woman. Her continual blood flow symbolized impurity (see Lev. 15:19–30). No one could touch her, and she could touch no one. When she walked through the marketplace, the law required her to shout aloud, "Unclean! Unclean!" so that people could scramble away and avoid touching her. Shopkeepers barred her from their stores. Townsfolk didn't invite her to their homes, or dinner tables, or the synagogue. She lived in loneliness, isolation, and misery. A sick woman without family or friends.

I often wonder about this woman's father and mother and brothers and sisters. They too would be required by society to shun her. They too would be rendered unclean, and unable to worship, if they came in skin contact with her. For twelve long years, the bleeding woman had been alone, unable to hug or be hugged, unable to touch or be touched. I wonder how long it had been since her own father had called her "daughter."

She had almost given up hope when she heard that Jesus, the healer-teacher, had arrived in Capernaum. She reckoned this was her last chance. She quietly slipped through the pressing crowds until she found him, and then she clutched his cloak. She believed that if she just touched the hem of his clothing, she would be healed. And she was right. The second she touched his robe, Jesus healed her. The terrible bleeding stopped.

But then something happened that surprised her. Jesus turned around suddenly and asked the crowd: "Who touched my clothes?" Trembling with fear, she quickly admitted her crime to Jesus. She fell at his feet, and waited for her inevitable punishment. She, an unclean woman, had dared to touch a holy man.

That's when Jesus, like a kind loving Father, looked at her tenderly, and spoke the one word her lonely heart had yearned to hear for a dozen years. "*Daughter*," Jesus said. "*Daughter*, your faith has healed you." Then Jesus blessed her: "Go in peace," he said, "and be freed from your suffering."

Within the word "daughter," Jesus clearly acknowledged his heavenly position. He and the Father were one. And this woman was his beloved daughter. It were as if he had said, "I love you; you are precious to me; I cherished you even before you were born; I will protect and guard you; I care when you hurt; I want to bring you peace and rest from your pain." It is important that she heard him say: "To society you are a 'common' woman, untouchable, and shunned by your family and friends. But to me you are special. No daughter of mine is 'common.' You can trust me with all your heart."

I like to believe that Jesus reunited the healed woman with her father, who likewise had suffered over the lost connection with his sick daughter. Perhaps, for many years to come, the woman, who now lived in good health and God's peace, heard once again her own father's beautiful words that began with the word "daughter."

Jesus, in his brief years on earth, showed us the face of our perfect heavenly Father—with his words, his actions, and his healings. He too shows you the face of your perfect heavenly Father as you study his Word and commune with him in prayer.

Daily Sunlight

Your Personal Time to Grow:

Read this woman's story in Mark 5:25–34. Also read Leviticus 12:2; 15:19–30. List those attributes shown by Jesus as Father to the bleeding woman. Of all these attributes, which ones speak most personally to you and why?

_____

_____

_____

_____

Although the biblical narrative stops after the woman's encounter with Jesus, this was just the beginning of the woman's story. Take a moment to think about what might have happened next. How do you imagine the woman's future differed from her past—physically, emotionally, relationally, spiritually?

_____

_____

_____

_____

_____

What wounds in your life keep you/kept you from being the daughter you most want to be?

_____

_____

_____

_____

Have you ever known a time when your father and/or family rejected you? If so, describe the impact it had on you.

_____

_____

_____

_____

What can you learn from the woman of Mark 5?

_____

_____

_____

_____

Your Personal Prayer:

Father, how happy I am that your inspired servant, Mark, inserted this brief story of the bleeding woman within the story of Jairus's daughter. I often feel like that bleeding woman who has no friends, and knows such isolation and loneliness. Speak to me throughout this Bible study, and allow me to learn from this biblical woman's example so that I too can find peace from my pain. In Jesus' name, amen.

Day 4: The affirming father

> "Then should not this woman, *a daughter of Abraham*, whom Satan has kept bound for eighteen long years, be set free on the Sabbath day from what bound her?"
>
> Jesus in Luke 13:16

Jesus knows the power of affirming a "daughter's" worth and value. Some of Jesus' harshest words erupt from his lips when the hypocritical Pharisees and synagogue leaders keep him from responding to, healing, and nurturing his suffering daughters. Luke tells us about a bent-over woman who comes to the synagogue on the Sabbath to worship God. A disease cripples her so severely that she cannot straighten up. If we could open the curtain that separates us by time and distance, and peek into the past, we might see her looking at the cold, stone synagogue floor. It is her sky. We might see her watching people who, without excuse, shuffle rudely and busily around her. She sees only their feet. Her body is pitifully and permanently bent at the waist. She can neither lie down flat, nor sit up straight. As a handicapped woman in that day and time, she lives with subhuman status, an outcast of society. She prays to God that he will heal her, petitioning him to repair her spine and return her to full-standing dignity—the respectful personhood she lost eighteen years ago.

When Jesus sees his disabled daughter, he immediately puts his hands on her and heals her. He gives her back her dignity. He restores her spine, and her place in society. She stands up straight. Strong and sturdy. She is no longer in-valid in the purpose-driven Jewish society.

Jesus' healing touch, however, brings caustic criticism from synagogue leaders. "There are six days for work," they shout. "So come and be healed on those days, not on the Sabbath" (Luke 13:14).

That's when Jesus puts them in their place. "You hypocrites!" he says. "Doesn't each of you on the Sabbath untie his ox or donkey from the stall and lead it out to give it water? Then should not this woman, a daughter of

Abraham, whom Satan has kept bound for eighteen long years, be set free on the Sabbath day from what bound her?" (vv. 15–16).

Jesus' words shock and humiliate the Pharisees—these arrogant sons of Abraham. Why? Because he refers to his daughter, the formerly crippled common woman, as a cherished and treasured and much-loved *daughter of Abraham*! He might have said it this way: "Sons of Abraham, this woman is your *sister*! As a *daughter* of Abraham, she too shares all your many high and lofty privileges that go with being a child of Abraham." He might have even added: "Boys, show your sister some respect! She is important and loved and valuable to Abraham and to God, her Father."

Jesus elevates this woman to the position of Abraham's "daughter." Scandalous! It is the *only* time in the *whole* Bible that *any* woman is *ever* called "a daughter of Abraham."

Nahash provides us with another example of a biblical dad who knew the importance of affirming a daughter. Scripture tells us that when Nahash's baby, Abigail, was born, he rejoiced. In fact, the name "Abigail" means "my father rejoiced." We aren't told much else about Nahash, the Ammonite ruler, except that he once befriended David (2 Sam. 10:1–2). Perhaps he passed his kindness and wisdom on to his daughter, for Abigail also wisely befriended David. And, in doing so, she saved the life of her rude, ill-bred husband, Nabal (whose name means "fool"). God later struck Nabal dead (1 Sam. 25:2–38), and David married Abigail. (Read the story of Abigail in 1 Sam. 25:2–42.)

Nahash's excitement over the birth of his daughter sounds much like my own dad's excitement when I was born. When the ambulance took my mother and me home (in the 1950s that was common practice), my dad left his car parked at the hospital and rode home in the ambulance so he could hold me. After he arrived home, he had to find a way to retrieve his car! I was told that story over and over again as a child, as an illustration of how my daddy treasured me from the moment I was born.

Author Gregory Lang describes his delight over the birth of his daughter: "When my wife told me she was pregnant I was overjoyed," he writes. "Something inside me told me that our child would be a girl. Throughout the pregnancy I referred to the baby as 'she'—never 'it'—and when we saw the first sonogram, I insisted that it was obviously a girl, even though the doctor said it was too early to tell. I was in the delivery room when she arrived. The first person she looked at was me. I was smitten instantly."[2]

Perhaps you also have a father who truly loves and cares for you. If so, you are fortunate. If not, you know the craving for affirmation from him. But, either way, know that you have a Father in heaven who is far greater than your human father. He is the forever Father, the life-giver, the healer of hurting women who so desperately need to hear again the precious name "daughter."

Daily Sunlight

Your Personal Time to Grow:

Read the crippled woman's entire story in Luke 13:10–17. If you could talk with her, what would you tell her about the power of a father's affirmation (or lack of it) in your life?

_____

_____

_____

_____

_____

Although human fathers are imperfect because they are created, fallen beings, and Jesus is perfect, in what ways does an affirming dad remind you of Jesus? What could a nonaffirming dad learn from Jesus' example?

_____

_____

_____

_____

_____

_____

What did this healed woman probably keep in her heart forever after her meeting with Jesus?

_____

_____

_____

Your Personal Prayer:

Father, in this story of the crippled woman, you have given me two gifts: a wonderful incident of your healing power, and a glimpse of your Father-hood — your incredible love for your daughters. I pray that, just as you affirmed the crippled woman in this story, I can recover from you the lost affirmation I never received from my father. Thank you for showing me that you, alone, are the perfect Father, the one who dearly loves me, your daughter. May I be a daughter who will make you proud. In the name of your Son, amen.

Day 5: The compassionate father

> Praise be to the God and Father of our Lord Jesus Christ, the Father of *compassion* and the God of all comfort, who comforts us in all our troubles.
>
> 2 Corinthians 1:3–4

God the Father is a compassionate Father even when our human father was/is not. Susie came to understand her heavenly Father's compassion later in her life—after she experienced a human father with no love, kindness, or consideration. Her father, who showed no compassion, taught Susie the meaning of the word. Susie tells her story:

"*Father of compassion.* What an oxymoron that phrase seemed to me. I'd read it countless times as a description of God the Father (2 Corinthians 1:3). But I knew the word *compassion* means 'to suffer with.' Although this phrase maintains that God the Father *suffered with me*, I've only known a father as one who *caused* me to suffer. Physical beatings, verbal berating and battering, cruel sarcasm and taunting—those are the things I associate with my father.

"For years I wondered if God the Father could be different. Could he actually suffer *with* me? Even if God did have the ability to be compassionate, why would he bother with me? I felt totally unlovable. Why else, I wondered, would my own father treat me with such blatant contempt?

"Yet I knew John 3:16 proclaimed God's love for the world. For several decades I struggled to believe that God could possibly love me. Then I finally figured it out—that verse *obligated* him to love me in a general way because I was part of the world. Yes, I belonged to him because I'd received the free gift of salvation through grace at age nine. But reality told me I was hardly a blip on the radar screen of God's attention. I was fortunate he chose to tolerate me. Expecting genuine love from him was more than I could ever hope.

"My childhood was a time of unending pain. The physical wounds of the beatings were nothing compared to the emotional scars of knowing my father found me so disgusting. Maybe good grades would make my father like me, or perhaps working harder at my chores. Surely he'd be glad I didn't drink, smoke, or become sexually involved as a teen.

"But nothing I did made a positive impact. I was convinced I was simply unlovable.

"If my own father could barely tolerate me, I reasoned, how could the heavenly Father—who actually *knew* all my sins—endure me? Surely he too was simply watching for a time to punish me. He may have been caught on the technicality of John 3:16, but I thought he cruelly watched my sins, just waiting to declare me unfit for the kingdom of God.

"Such fear drove me to try harder not to sin, to pray longer, to serve tirelessly in my church, to study the Bible and memorize Scripture, to try to appease the *angry* God responsible for my life or death. I became an overachiever, diligently working to earn my salvation and keep God's anger at bay.

"No matter how much theology I learned, I always thought I had to appease God. Despite what Scripture said, I viewed him as in control, giving commands, and expecting me to measure up. The effort toward living a godly life seemed my responsibility alone. The fear and guilt were never-ending.

"In desperation, I turned to Christian counseling. It helped me some, but the spiritual ramifications of my childhood were still paramount.

"As I continued seeking God, he patiently continued drawing me to himself. I'll never forget the day I heard him speak to my spirit, 'You're totally accepted in the Son.' It was a gift I'd never expected to receive. Such assurance! My relationship with God truly was a gift of Christ. Although I now realized I no longer needed to earn my place with God, I still worked endlessly. But the deep fear was gradually losing its grip.

"As I began reading new translations of Scripture, God deepened my thirst for himself. His Word became alive with passion as I read of his enduring love for me. I began to view God in a new light, realizing he was more intent on seeking me than I'd ever been in responding. I scoured the Bible, looking for every verse that spoke of his love. I absorbed every text that described the value he placed on me. I drank in every word of Living Water to quench my insatiable thirst. God became a real and personally involved being in my life.

"God was succeeding in convincing me intellectually that he was so different from the caricature I had carried from early childhood. As I began viewing him as a kind and loving Father, I confessed my sin of unbelief in his goodness. His kindness truly was leading me to repentance (Rom. 2:4).

"God was transforming my attitude from viewing him as cruel and vengeful to seeing him as someone deeply interested in my life. But I still had questions. If God truly loved me, why had he permitted my childhood to be a time of such terror? Where had he been as I suffered degradation and shame? If he'd abandoned me when I was a helpless child, could I, as an adult, trust him?

"These questions plagued my spiritual journey. But in his grace and timing, God continued opening doors for me. In his sovereignty, God led me to a group of people who encouraged me to bring my questions to God. As I poured out my grief and pain, they responded with compassion, literally suffering with me.

"Their example encouraged me toward believing that God too was filled with compassion for me. Over many months, God began showing me that he had been present as Immanuel, *God with us*, throughout my life. Time after time, he comforted me with his presence as I cried out with pain from the past. Repeatedly he reassured me emotionally through the caring presence of two dear Christian women who prayed for me.

"As I went to God honestly, and believing that he would receive my questions, I was released from the lies I'd believed about God's nature. My spiritual eyes were healed from the blindness that had kept me in darkness. I was freed from the captivity of the past. Truly, I was finding that the time of the Lord's favor had come.

"*Father of compassion?* How gladly I now embrace that phrase as so true of the heavenly Father. I now see that God is not merely loving, but is truly love personified (1 John 4:8, 16) because his very nature is love. All he does is prompted by love.

"God is love—and that extends even to me. Not only has God changed my perception of him, he's changed my perception of myself. I now understand I was worth his sacrifice on Calvary because he placed value on me. Such worth is pure gift from him, nothing I could ever earn—nor do I ever need to earn. Salvation is a gift of God's grace.

"I now realize that because God is pure love, he's constantly working to draw his children into an ever-deepening relationship of intimacy with him. Polite and aloof relationships may work in some circles, but God is far more interested in giving each of us a relationship of deeply experienced love (see Eph. 3:14–21).

"What about my biological father? The most amazing thing has occurred. Since God has been at work immersing me in his love, I find myself being filled with compassion for my father! This man, who once caused so much suffering in my life, is now a focus of God's compassion working in and through me. This too comes from God. I, in no way, could ever have created this unexpected gift.

"Years ago I was intellectually able to forgive my father (although for years I had never expected to be able to forgive). But I now find that God's love has taken me to a new level of forgiveness. I still grieve the pain of my childhood. But I now find myself grieving more for the man who was the source of my pain. I now literally *suffer with him* over the tragedy of his own life.

"God has genuinely given me a love for my father I never would have believed possible. In fact, because I know my heart, I'm aware that, if several years ago anyone had suggested I could have such love for him, I would have rejected the thought and the love as something my father didn't deserve. But what an awesome God who can give the gift of love!

"God amazes me. He isn't merely loving—he's pure love. He isn't simply kind—he's total kindness. He isn't just good—he's complete goodness. He is the personification of the fruit of the Spirit (Gal. 5:22–23).

"In my experience, I've discovered that Jesus is a good and loving Savior who's come to set captives free. By his grace, he proclaims, 'My purpose is to give life in all its fullness' (John 10:10 NLT). How grateful I am that his grace includes me."

As we have seen this week, good fathers teach, sacrifice and care for, affirm, and show compassion to their daughters. While no father, except God, is perfect, dads can give their daughters gifts of love and encouragement that make huge differences in their lives, their marriages, and their own parenting. In this reading's "Daily Sunlight," let's talk for a moment about your dad.

Daily Sunlight

Your Personal Time to Grow:

During this week, you have seen some of the wonderful traits that good dads have shown their daughters. You read about Cokiesha's dad and what he taught her about God and life. You read about Jairus and how his personal sacrifice and active concern saved his dying daughter's life. You also saw how Jesus, as the perfect "Abba"—our heavenly Father, reached out in love, healing, tenderness, and affirmation to the bleeding woman and the crippled woman. And you saw how Susie's dad—a cold, uncaring man—taught her the true meaning of compassion and kindness. Take a few minutes and briefly review Day 1 through Day 5's devotionals.

Make a list of all those things you learned that you did not know before you read this chapter.

_____

_____

_____

_____

_____

What most impressed you about the father-daughter relationship and its continuing effect on adult women?

_____

_____

_____

_____

Now look in detail at some of the godly attributes human dads can possess, as provided by a group of women I surveyed. From the list, circle all those attributes your father possessed. Then put an "x" beside all those attributes you wished your father possessed.

Affectionate	Generous	Kind	Loving	Fun
Enjoys family	Loves God	Works hard	Intelligent	Supportive
Honest	Friendly	Knowledgeable	Dependable	Trustworthy
Good character	Respectable	Good leader	Physically fit	Loyal
Self-disciplined	Responsible	Understanding	Good listener	Well-respected
Self-starter	Loves wife	Loves mother	Improves self	Sympathetic
Goal-oriented	Tender	Communicates	Gentle	Has patience
Perseveres	Finishes tasks	Reaches goals	Spiritual leader	Sense of humor
Clear goals	Kind-hearted	Helps others	Wise	Self-confident
Easy to talk to	Warm to others	Considerate	Accepting	Even-tempered
Stable	Pleasant	Listens	Encourages	Is sensitive
Humble	Spiritually sound	Easy-going	Available	Apologizes when wrong
Asks for forgiveness	Accepts apologies	Forgives	Builds up family	Compliments family
Helpful	Smiles often	Takes blame when necessary	Soft-spoken	Interesting
Sacrificing	Affirming	Caring	Teaching	Compassionate

Envision your childhood as a garden. Name the "good plants" your father planted in your garden. Describe the plants in a creative way. Tell how you felt about each one. (For example: "My dad planted roses in my garden. Roses are beautiful and fragrant. I love the delicacy and colors of a newly bloomed rose.") As you imagine the garden of your adulthood, list the good plants that still grow there. If you choose to, find a box of crayons or colored pencils, and on a separate piece of plain paper draw a picture of your garden as it might have looked in your childhood, in your adolescence, and in your adulthood. (The art may be elementary. You need not show it to anyone. It's just for you.)

_____

_____

_____

_____

_____

_____

_____

Did your father teach you anything about God? If so, what is most meaningful to you now? If not, what do you wish your father had taught you about God?

_____

_____

_____

_____

Week 1 has been a time to remember your human father's good points, and "a time to keep" his godly attributes in your heart and thoughts. During Week 2, you and I will examine some biblical and modern fathers (like Susie's dad) who have not exhibited godly attributes toward their daughters, and who have distorted their daughters' views of God.

Your Personal Prayer:

Dear Jesus, thank you for my human father (or my father-substitute). I know that all humans are imperfect, but I thank you that my dad possessed all those godly attributes I listed. Please allow me to forever keep those wonderful qualities close to my heart and always in my thoughts. I love and admire him most for his _____.

I also pray for the world's fathers, that they may be loving and godly dads to all the earth's daughters. May each daughter alive learn about you, dear heavenly Parent, through the godly actions and words of her human parents. Be close to all the world's children who have no living fathers. Provide someone dear in their lives — a father figure — who will teach them about you. In Jesus' name, amen.

Your Weekly Feeding—Group Bible Study

"A Time to Keep"

Growing Together in God's Word:

1. Briefly share a highlight from the Week 1 "Daily Sunlight" section, something that particularly spoke to you.

2. Read John 6:46 and 10:30. What do these verses tell you about Jesus' relationship to his Father? Why is his relationship to God so essential to our salvation?

   _____

   _____

3. Read John 14:1–2, 6–7, 9–10. What promise does Jesus make in this Scripture? How do these verses comfort you in your own relationship to the Father?

   _____

   _____

4. Read Luke 23:34. What was Jesus' last request of the Father? Compare and contrast this instance of forgiveness with any you have offered or might have to offer.

   _____

   _____

5. Jesus called his Father "Abba." This Greek word is used only three times in the New Testament: Mark 14:36; Romans 8:15; and Galatians 4:6. Read these verses, then answer the following questions:

a. How is the name "Abba" used in the Scripture readings?

_____

b. What name did you call your earthly father when you were a child? What do you call your father now?

_____

c. From your own experience with your heavenly Father, which of God's attributes are most meaningful to you?

_____

d. Describe an instance of how you already are displaying this attribute (these attributes) in your own life, or how you might start.

_____

Group Prayer:

[Pray together aloud and in unison] My God, we want to have with you the trusting, loving relationship Jesus had with you. We also want to call you "Abba." Show us through your Holy Spirit how we, your daughters, can know you intimately. In the name of your Son, amen.

Week 2: A Time to Throw Away

Day 1: The problem of flawed fathers

> The greater the degree of dysfunction (or poor modeling) in a family,
> the greater the potential for emotional, spiritual, and relational wounds.
> Put another way, the poorer the parental model we have of God's love,
> forgiveness, and power, the harder time we have experiencing and
> applying these characteristics in our lives.
>
> Robert S. McGee, *Search for Significance*

Many women today have fathers who didn't model God's example of love, forgiveness, and power. Perhaps your father didn't model these qualities of God's character either. You might have had a father who neglected you or severely criticized you. As a child, you may have even known the deeper wounds of abuse and abandonment. Good fathers are hard to find. Even God's Word records only a handful of fathers who adequately represented God to their children.

In this chapter, we'll look at some of Scripture's flawed fathers and the impact they left on their daughters. Did you know that "the Bible shows us more failure than success in the foibles of its human fathers, even though the failure of fathers to reflect God's character often distorts a child's view of God himself"?[1] The problem of flawed fathers has hurt children throughout history. Perhaps you too were hurt as a child.

Lot, Abraham's nephew, receives my award for "Worst Father of World History." What he did was cruel and unimaginable. The story starts well enough. Lot invited two male visitors to Sodom (who were really angels) into his home and generously cooked them a meal. Before the evening ended, however, the wicked city's evil, perverse men surrounded Lot's house, demanding that he give them the two men so they could "have sex with them" (Gen. 19:5). Lot stepped outside and tried to make a deal. He told them they couldn't have his guests. After all, the host's job was to protect them. But he said: "Look, I have two daughters who have never slept with a man. Let me bring them out to you, and you can do what you like with them" (v. 8).

I've read this passage many times and it still sends chills down my spine. Can you imagine the horror that leaped into the minds of Lot's daughters?

What kind of father offers his virgin daughters to a gang of rapists! Fortunately, the angels intervened, pulled Lot back into the house, and struck with blindness the warped men outside.

Later, when God destroyed the sinful cities of Sodom and Gomorrah, he spared Lot and his two daughters, who found refuge in a mountain cave. But what happened to the unloved girls? They deceived their flawed father. They each wanted to have a baby, but all the men they knew had been killed by the burning sulfur God rained down upon them (vv. 24, 28). So one night the girls schemed to get their father drunk on wine. Then each daughter slept with him. Incest. Both women became pregnant. Nine months later, each bore a baby.

For all his good points, King David proved to be another flawed father. When his son Amnon deceived and raped David's virgin daughter, Tamar (Amnon's half sister), David became furious. Yet he did nothing, ignoring the crime. Rape ruined Tamar's chances of marriage and motherhood. She moved in with her brother, Absalom, and lived her entire life "a desolate woman" (2 Sam. 13:20). And Absalom, not David, eventually settled the score, albeit savagely. He avenged Tamar's rape by killing Amnon. (See all of 2 Samuel 13 for the entire story.)

Another biblical father, Jacob, had his flaws too. Jacob's quiver was full of boys, but did you know he also had a daughter, Dinah? We hear a lot about Jacob's sons, especially Joseph, the one he unfairly favored over his eleven other sons, the one he intentionally spoiled (Gen. 37:3–4). "Probably, little celebration occurred at Dinah's birth since she was a girl," writes Rhonda Harrington Kelley. "The Scriptures do not explain Dinah's name as they do for male children."[2] (See Gen. 30:21.) Like David's daughter, Tamar, a violent rape also ruined Dinah's life. Dinah's brothers, Simeon and Levi, took revenge on her rapist, Shechem, killing and kidnapping and plundering his entire city (Gen. 34). On his deathbed, Jacob cursed his two sons for their needless brutality (49:5–7).

In each of these examples, a daughter or daughters suffered devastating results. It's the same today. An unloved and mistreated daughter carries a lifetime of scars due to her father's abuse. The abuse affects every part of her life—her marriage, her parenting, her career, her faith, and her self-esteem.

During the next nine days, I will introduce you to contemporary women who have suffered due to a faulty father. Perhaps you will identify with some of these women. Or maybe your mother, friend, or coworker has suffered in similar ways. If so, know that God offers you, and the hurting women you know, hope for the future. You need not suffer any longer. The time has come to "throw away" father-caused pain and its devastating results.

Daily Sunlight

Your Personal Time to Grow:

Read Ecclesiastes 3:1–8. Solomon mentions various activities: birth and death, planting and uprooting, killing and healing, tearing down and building up, weeping and laughing, mourning and dancing, scattering stones and gathering stones, embracing and refraining from embracing, searching and giving up the search, keeping and throwing away, tearing and mending, speaking and silence, loving and hating, warring and celebrating peace. As you look at this list of activities, write down the things that most describe your life so far. (For instance: I have spent a large portion of my life weeping and mourning. I speak far more than I listen, or am silent. I've hated many people, and I have spent little time loving others.)

_____

_____

_____

_____

_____

Read the tragic story of Tamar's rape and Absalom's revenge (2 Samuel 13, especially verses 20–21.) Have you or someone close to you ever experienced a trauma like Tamar endured? If so, how did you or your loved one get through the situation? What consequences awaited the abuser?

_____

_____

_____

_____

Describe other events in your life that left you as devastated—weeping, mourning, tearing, hating—as Tamar's rape left her. How did you cope with them? In what ways do you still suffer from their memories?

_____

_____

_____

_____

_____

Tamar's father, David, failed her after her trauma. Have you ever experienced a time when your father failed you? If so, explain. What was the impact of his action/inaction on you?

_____

_____

_____

_____

Your Personal Prayer:

My Jesus, I feel gratitude to you for allowing me to read the past stories of women in pain. Help me to learn from them so that I can look to their examples for guidance in my life. Teach me, Lord, how to rise above a parent's brutality and neglect, and find freedom and peace in you, my perfect Father. In Jesus' name, amen.

Week 2: A Time to Throw Away

Day 2: Alexandra's father, the controlling dad

> True friendship and intimacy cannot exist in a relationship where one person is a controller and the other is a pleaser. Neither person is willing to be open and vulnerable.
>
> H. Norman Wright, *Always Daddy's Girl*

Throughout history, many of the world's daughters have suffered under controlling and abusive fathers. In ancient Rome, for instance, fathers had absolute *property* rights over their families. Called *patria potestas* ("the father's power"), the law stated that a man could make his children marry and divorce, could disown his children and sell them into slavery, and could even kill his wife and children. By law, a man's family became his personal chattel.

"When a child was born, the child was placed between the father's feet. If the father picked up the child, the child stayed in the home. If the father turned and walked away, the child was either left to die or taken to the forum and sold at auction. Most children auctioned away at birth were raised to work as prostitutes or slaves."[3]

In some families today, fathers still "rule the roost" *patria potestas*-style. And their daughters suffer a lifetime because of their unkind control. Author Tim Kimmel writes: "I believe it's safe to assume God never intended one person to control another. He didn't wire us to respond well to it, either. In each of our hearts is an innate aversion to a person . . . compelling us to do things that primarily benefit them."[4]

Controlling fathers can ruin a daughter's life. Norma Jeane Mortenson/ Baker, later known as actress Marilyn Monroe, shows us an example of a father's ruthless control. She lived the first seven years of her life with a controlling foster father, Albert Bolender. Marilyn's biological father deserted her unmarried mother, Gladys. Mental problems kept Gladys from caring for her newborn daughter. Research on Gladys's family tree shows that she likewise suffered under a seriously flawed father (Otis Elmer Monroe) and grandfather (Jacob Monroe). Otis Monroe showed erratic behavior, drank heavily, and, due to his careless womanizing, suffered from syphilis. Like Gladys, Otis spent considerable time in a mental institution.[5] A desperate and troubled man, granddad Jacob Monroe killed himself in 1872.[6]

Not only did Marilyn come out of a dysfunctional family, but she ended up in one as well. Marilyn's foster parents, the Bolenders, "were terribly strict," she remembers. "They brought me up harshly."[7] After her stint with the Bolenders, Marilyn lived for two years in the Los Angeles Orphan's Home. That's when her mother's friend, Grace McKee, brought nine-year-old Marilyn into her own home to live. Grace treated Marilyn kindly. She was "the first person who ever patted my head or touched my cheek," Marilyn remembers. I "still remember how thrilled I felt when her kind hand touched me."[8]

Unfortunately, Marilyn had suffered significant damage by then. She spent the rest of her brief life in and out of marriages and high on drugs, feeling unloved and unwanted, always looking for love and acceptance. Hollywood proved no kinder than her foster father. "Hollywood is a place where they'll pay you a thousand dollars for a kiss and fifty cents for your soul," she once said.[9] On August 5, 1962, she died from a drug overdose, ultimately a victim, like her mother, of generations of men who controlled them.

Let me introduce you to Alexandra. Alexandra, like Marilyn, grew up with a controlling father. He took absolute authority over every area of Alexandra's life.

"My dad—a power-hungry controller—ruled our home like he ruled his workplace—with an iron fist. I feared him. My smallest mistake brought severe punishment, usually a beating with his belt. He made all the decisions for the family. He asked no one to contribute ideas about home, travel, vacations, purchases, or anything else. My poor mother took on the role of servant around our house. She voiced no opinion. She offered no input. She just quietly obeyed the orders my drill-sergeant dad dished out."

Alexandra's father used money to control his wife, Martha, and his daughter. He alone held the purse strings. And he held them tightly. He spent megabucks on his "big-boy toys," but dribbled money out a dime at a time to Martha and Alexandra. Martha saved a little grocery money each week to pay for her prescription medicines. She also sewed her own clothes since her husband refused her money to buy them. Martha had no idea how much income her husband made, nor the amount of life insurance he carried.

Alexandra's father also used conditional love to control his family. When Alexandra brought home an A+ on her report card, her father expressed something resembling affection. But anything less than A+ brought a certain look from him, one of disgust and disappointment. His harsh criticism lasted for days. The scowl stayed on his face for as long as a week, during which time he hardly spoke. Alexandra "did somersaults" to try to please her never-satisfied dad. She yearned for affection she didn't have to earn. She became a perfectionist, always struggling to please him in every way.

In his book *Women Who Try Too Hard: Breaking the Pleaser Habits*, Dr. Kevin Leman describes fathers like Alexandra's as "flaw pickers."

> The flaw pickers are perfectionistic parents who are strong on discipline, performance, and criticism.... The flaw-picking parent makes everything the child is and does a matter of endless concern. What happens to the daughter of a flaw-picker?
>
> The result is that the child grows into adulthood, taking along an inner child of the past who is always whispering, "You can do better, you should do better, you ought to do better, you aren't up to standard." More often than not, suicidal teenagers have flaw-picking parents.[10]

After Alexandra's experience with her father, you'd think she'd run from men who sought to dominate her. But quite the opposite happened. During her dating days, she was drawn—like a moth to a flame—to male controllers. In fact, Alexandra married a man far more controlling than her father ever dared to be. She continued her perfection-pleasing habits throughout her married life. If she spent too much money on groceries, her husband withdrew his affection. If she disagreed with his opinions, he became a "silent knight" and clammed up for days. She tried every way possible to please him. But she couldn't please him anymore than she could please her father.

Controllers can cause their daughters to do one of two things: buckle under and become a people-pleaser, or withdraw from life. Some women cannot handle what they consider failure. They withdraw completely through suicide. Failing to please a controlling husband or father leaves them exhausted and disillusioned. They just quit trying. When women become people-pleasers, they give up their unique individuality and become like Jello in society's mold. They let themselves be poured and formed into unnatural shapes. They become actors whose self-esteem is based on their performance. They wear masks and play hypocritical roles.

And how do the Alexandras of this world view God the Father? As a brutal taskmaster, a heavenly "flaw-picker," who loves them when they're "good," and who withdraws his love when they're "bad." To them, God reveals himself through Scripture in the "thou shalt not" verses. Somehow the Alexandras of this world just can't believe that God loves them for who they are—his unique and individually gifted daughters—the special women he made them to be.

"If God the Father is anything like my human father," Alexandra admits, "I don't want anything to do with him. It's hard enough trying to please a 'flaw-picking' father and husband. I certainly don't want a heavenly Father who has the power to zap me with a lightning bolt when I don't measure up!"

"Alexandra," I yearn to say, "you are a perfectionist-pleaser because your human father based his love on your performance. He loved you with a conditional love, a pseudo-love, dependent on how your behavior affected him. But God your heavenly Father loves you with an unconditional love. He loves you for who you are, not for what you do and don't do."

If you, like Alexandra and Marilyn Monroe, have been the victim of a controlling dad, I want to say the same thing to you: with your heavenly Father's help, you can throw away those perfectionistic habits; you can quit trying to please everybody; and you can allow your heavenly Father to build up your damaged self-esteem. You can become the beautiful individual God gifted you to be, and enjoy an intimate relationship with him—your perfect loving Father. (On Day 1 of Week 4, we'll talk about how God loves you unconditionally.)

Daily Sunlight

Your Personal Time to Grow:

Read Ecclesiastes 3:9–14. Solomon believes that God "has made everything beautiful in its time." In what ways has God created and brought beauty into your life? What are some of the good gifts that God has given you?

_____

_____

_____

_____

Read Ephesians 3:17–19. In this Scripture passage, Paul describes Christ's love. What do Paul's words mean to you when he writes that this love surpasses knowledge?

_____

_____

_____

Did you grow up with a dad like Alexandra's? If so, how did his domination impact you? Or perhaps you know another woman in your family, church, work, school, or community who endured the harsh domination of a controlling parent. How did his control influence her adult life?

_____

_____

_____

_____

During the next two weeks, you will be offered two prayers to pray. Please choose the prayer that best fits your situation.

Your Personal Prayer #1:

[Pray this prayer only if your father was like Alexandra's father] My precious Lord, I have grown up with a controlling father like Alexandra's. I can understand her pain because I also have experienced this same pain. Please uproot all the damage that my dad's control caused me. I pray for my father, and I trust that you will show me how to forgive him. In the name of your Son, amen.

Your Personal Prayer #2:

Father, I pray for all those women who have had harsh and controlling parents. Allow them to know the beauty of your love, a love given to them without condition, a love not based on performance. Help them to discover your total love and acceptance as recorded in your Holy Word. Help me to carry your good news of unconditional love to them so that they may know you as "Abba." In Jesus' name, amen.

Week 2: A Time to Throw Away

Day 3: Bethany's father, the unapproachable dad

> Underparenting dads place kids low on the ladder of priorities. Even when they're home—which doesn't tend to be a big priority—these dads are often someplace else mentally and emotionally.
>
> Kevin Leman, *Making Sense of the Men in Your Life*

Bethany's dad, Ralph, provided her with a comfortable home, a private-school education, nice clothes, and good food. He never criticized her, nor did he base his love on her performance. But Ralph had a major flaw. He ignored his daughter. Bethany felt like a stranger to him. Most of the time he was there physically, but never emotionally. After her father died, Bethany realized that she knew very little about him.

"Chronically AWOL is my label for neglectful parents who check out on their children in one way or another. . . . In many cases, however, a parent lives in the home with the child but is really 'absent' as far as being interested in the child in any real sense."[11]

"As a child and young adult," admits Bethany, "I craved my father's attention. I wanted him to look me in the eye every now and then, and to listen to my opinions, hurts, and problems. But he wouldn't. Oh, once in a while, he'd give me a lecture, especially when I disobeyed him or smarted off to my mom. But he'd never just sit down and talk to me. I longed to share my dreams with him, to hear him talk about life and love. I begged him to tell me about his childhood, his family, his college days, his military experiences, and his friends. But he revealed nothing about himself. I feel as if I lived eighteen years with a stranger. Like his heart was wrapped in concrete. I just couldn't break through all the barriers he put up."

"Unfortunately, many fathers are emotionally distant, insensitive, or cold," writes Charles Sell. "During the early part of the 20th century, traditional fathers focused on authority and power. They were the disciplinarians and breadwinners, not the nurturers. They left nurturing to mothers. Men thought they had to be tough rather than tender. One expert calls these dads 'fathers with fangs.'"[12] Bethany's father had no fangs, but he had no tenderness either. He sat at the breakfast and supper table every day, but he remained emotionally distant, insensitive, and cold.

Bethany's father was unapproachable to her. At breakfast, Bethany usually stared at the back of the newspaper Ralph read. At supper, the blaring television occupied his total attention. He rarely spoke to Bethany except to correct her table manners. Even on their rare family vacations, Ralph drove the car, listened to the radio, and hardly spoke a word.

"I never remember just sitting down at the kitchen table and having a heart-to-heart conversation with him," Bethany cries. "It's like he just didn't care about me."

Bethany remembers a special night at a friend's house. "One night my next-door neighbor had a slumber party for me and a few little friends. After all of us youngsters dressed in pajamas and settled into one big bed, her dad came into the room, sat on the bed, and just talked to us. He told us about his childhood on a farm, how he used to milk cows early in the mornings, how he used to chase chickens around the coop. We laughed together as he told us about funny things that had happened that day at his job. He even told us bedtime stories. After he said 'goodnight' and turned out the lights, I asked my friend a question. 'Susie, does your dad talk to you like that every night?' With a surprised look on her face, she answered me: 'Of course he does! Doesn't yours?' I wondered for years afterward why my daddy didn't do that.

"Two significant things happened after I turned eighteen," Bethany remembers. "I left home to start college, and my dad died of a massive heart attack. I suffered from a deep 'father-hunger.' My 'love bank' registered empty. I understand now why I became promiscuous, why I hopped from one guy's bed to another trying to find a man who would show me the love and attention I craved. I never found that man. During my senior year of college, I married an older man, Larry, who at first showed me great attention and whispered into my ear all the 'sweet-love-words' I needed to hear. After the honeymoon, however, his true self came out. He began to act a whole lot like my dad. Withdrawn. Distant. Cold. He lives in his own world now, a world where I'm not welcomed. I know little about my husband's background, thoughts, feelings, dreams, or anything else. He provides financially well for me and the children, but his heart and mind are those of a stranger's."

Why did Bethany choose a husband who was so much like her father? It's hard to understand, but many (if not most) women will inevitably choose a husband who has the same flaws as her father. That's one reason why the father-daughter experience is so important. "The relationship between a daughter and her father is crucial. I believe it has lifelong effects and repercussions," writes Kevin Leman. "Daughters who have negative experiences with Daddy because he is distant and unaffectionate, or because he leaves through death, divorce, or desertion, will find themselves drawn to the very same kind of man when they are ready for marriage."[13]

Sometimes women, like Bethany, think they don't deserve anyone better. They also may find comfort in familiar habits. Relating to a husband like she has related to her father—even with major flaws—can seem more comfortable for most women.

Bethany's father also greatly influenced her belief in God. In her sophomore year of college, Bethany's friend Julie told her about God. Julie described her own loving, intimate relationship with God, and she invited Bethany to come to him too. But Bethany couldn't fathom an intimate relationship with anyone she addressed as "father." Bethany believed her heavenly Father was as distant and unapproachable as her human father.

Author Dee Clark writes about growing up with her own emotionally distant father: "All the years I was growing up," she admits, " I never really knew how to talk to him, and he really didn't know how to talk to me! We were like two strangers walking side by side on a crowded street. When I was with him, nothing was there!"[14]

As an adult, Dee and her father became even more distant. Dee often wished that she "could go back to the way things were when I was a child. I wished we could be a family again and that I could know what it was like to have a dad who was there for me."[15]

Dee's story reminds me of Thornton Wilder's play *Our Town*. The main character, Emily, dies at age twenty-six, while giving birth. As the "dead" Emily sits in a solitary chair on the bare stage, she begs the narrator/stage manager to let her revisit her childhood so she could look her parents in the eye and hope that they would look back and really "see" her. The stage manager grants her wish, and allows her to choose one day from her childhood that she most wanted to relive. Emily chose her twelfth birthday: February 11, 1899.

Alive again, Emily first sees her mother and family.

"I can't bear it," she cries. "They're so young and beautiful. Why did they ever have to get old?"

Then she shouts: "Mama, I'm here. I'm grown up. I love you all, everything—I can't look at everything hard enough."[16]

Emily turns to the stage manager and says: "I can't go on. It goes so fast. We don't have time to look at one another."

She breaks down and sobs: "I didn't realize. So all that was going on and we never noticed. Take me back—up the hill—to my grave. But first: Wait! One more look."

Emily looks again at life. She says good-bye to Mama and Papa, to clocks ticking and sunflowers growing, to food and coffee, newly ironed dresses and hot baths, to sleeping and waking up. "Oh, earth," she cries out, "you're too wonderful for anybody to realize you."

Through tears, she asks the stage manager: "Do any human beings ever realize life while they live it?—every every minute?"

The stage manager pauses, and then says: "The saints and poets, maybe— they do some."[17]

By withdrawing emotionally, Bethany's dad missed the wonder and joy of watching his daughter grow up. Bethany also missed out. She felt as if she didn't matter to her father. She entered adult life with a "father-hunger" that has lasted her entire lifetime. Left with a void in her heart, she needs to know that God can fill that void. He is not uninvolved and distant, but kind, loving, and approachable.

I yearn to tell Bethany that God the Father wants an intimate relationship with his precious daughter. That he is but a prayer away from her all the time. That he listens to her when she prays. Bethany has much pain to sort through and many wrong beliefs to gather up and throw out. If Bethany doesn't stop to examine her thoughts, actions, and ideas, she will remain sad and lonely. She will continue to crave the attention and loving affection of a man, to nurse a well-deep hole in her soul, and to feel like she just doesn't matter.

Perhaps you also grew up with an emotionally distant, uninvolved father. Maybe you believe you just don't matter to him or to your heavenly Father. If so, perhaps you wonder if you can find hope for the intimacy needed to fill the void in your heart. Know that you can. (On Day 2 of Week 4, we'll see that God is kind, compassionate, and always approachable.)

Daily Sunlight

Your Personal Time to Grow:

Read Ecclesiastes 3:15–22. Have you ever felt like Solomon when he wrote about society's wickedness, the seeming meaninglessness of life, and the destiny of each person—death? Have you ever resented God because he allows wickedness and pain on earth? If so, explain.

Read Isaiah 54:8 and Ephesians 2:6–7. How do these Scripture verses relate to your own story?

How does God most express his loving-kindness to you?

Respond to this statement: "Open lines of communication and the modes of communicating are the single most essential tool for the health and depth of the father-adolescent daughter relationship."[18] Describe your "communication lines" with your dad during your childhood, during your adolescence. Did he build a close father-daughter relationship with you through communication, and if so, how did he do this?

_____

_____

_____

_____

Have you ever felt like Bethany—like you have a "well-deep hole in your soul"? Have you ever craved the love, attention, and eye-to-eye intimacy that Bethany craves? If so, please explain.

_____

_____

_____

If you could revisit your childhood for one day, like Emily does in _Our Town_, which day would you choose and why?

_____

_____

_____

_____

Your Personal Prayer #1:

[Pray this prayer only if your father was like Bethany's dad] Jesus, I have grown up with a cold, unapproachable parent like Bethany's. I can understand Bethany's pain because I have experienced this same pain. Please uproot all the damage my dad's emotional distance has caused me. I pray for my father, and I ask you to show me how to forgive him. In the name of your Son, amen.

Your Personal Prayer #2:

Father, I pray for all those women like Bethany, who yearn for love and close communication with a human dad. Show the Bethanys of this world how you can fill the hole in their soul with your kindness, compassion, and love. Let them experience your abundant availability and approachability. Let them know that you are involved in every aspect of their lives, that you love them so much you even keep count of the hairs on their heads (Matt. 10:31). In Jesus' name, amen.

Week 2: A Time to Throw Away

Day 4: Joyce's father, the overparenting dad

> A dad who overparents will eventually smother his daughter. He's positive
> he knows how his little girl should turn out, and he'll raise her to be like
> a seal that claps its flippers when Daddy holds out a fishy little morsel.
> When this happens, she will always seek her daddy's ever-elusive approval
> and have little or no confidence in herself.
>
> Kevin Leman, *Making Sense of the Men in Your Life*

Unlike Bethany's emotionally distant dad who underparented her, Joyce's father became too involved in her life. He overparented her. He made all her decisions—both big and small. He took her shopping and chose her clothes. He decided which college she would attend and what her major would be. He interviewed her friends—both male and female—before she stepped into their cars for a brief afternoon outing. For twenty-six years, until her father died, Joyce had no free will of her own. He ruled almost every minute of her life.

Joyce's childhood and adolescence reminds me of a multicolored bird—a *sun couner*—I saw in a family-owned drugstore. When I walked into the store, I noticed the bird sitting on a perch by the front door, neither caged nor chained. I watched as people opened the door and came in and out. The bird could have escaped into the cloudless blue sky of freedom countless times. Yet he remained unmoved.

I was amazed. "Why doesn't he fly away?" I asked the owner. "Is he sick? Can't he fly?"

"Oh sure, he can fly! He's perfectly healthy!" he told me. "But, you see, when he was a baby, we clipped his wings real short. Whenever they started to grow out, and he was tempted to fly away, we'd clip 'em short again. Now we don't have to clip his wings anymore. He just sits there all day and doesn't make a sound. Guess he just never realized he could fly."

Joyce has also never realized that she can fly. Grown, married, and with children, she still can't make everyday decisions on her own. Her father never taught her she could think with her own brain. Instead, he did all her thinking for her.

"A father-teacher knows that unless his daughter learns how to make decisions, and understands and even suffers the appropriate consequences herself, she will not grow into healthy womanhood. She will constantly be looking for others to decide for her."[19]

Joyce rarely makes an important decision. "I put them off. I procrastinate until someone else makes the decision for me, or until, by failing to make a decision, I've already made the decision. When I do 'bite the bullet' and decide one way or the other, I spend weeks second-guessing myself: Did I make a good choice? Did I make a bad choice? I guess if my dad were alive, he'd still be making my decisions for me.

"Daddy was over-involved in my life. I guess he didn't trust me, or he was afraid I'd get kidnapped or hurt or something. Maybe he just didn't think I had good sense and he had to supervise me full-time. At any rate, I had no freedom as a child or teen. When I did go somewhere without him, like on a movie date with friends or to a restaurant with a boyfriend, Daddy gave me strict orders to call him once every hour. He said he just wanted to know where I was and that I was okay. Even after I married, Daddy called several times a day to 'check on me.'

"Daddy's family meant a lot to him. He made sure I knew Jesus as my Lord and Savior. He took me to church—every time the doors opened. I was involved in everything—Sunday school, youth groups, church camps, youth choirs, and Vacation Bible School. Daddy gave me deep roots in family and faith, but he never gave me wings. He was kind and loving like a shepherd. But, instead of letting me walk on my own two feet, he (emotionally) 'put me on his back and carried me.' He wouldn't let me make my own mistakes or experience life. Sometimes I think he 'crippled' me so I would always have to depend on him.

"Our big 'blow-up' happened when I finished my junior year of high school. I had been rather compliant until Daddy told me the college I 'had' to attend. Located near my neighborhood, the college would allow me to live at home. But I wanted to go away to college, and find some freedom from Daddy's over-protection and rules. But he wouldn't hear of it. He told me firmly: 'Joyce, if you want me to pay for your college education, you'll go where I say you'll go and you'll live where I say you'll live!' And that was the end of that. I had no money to pay for college. Oh, I fussed a little, and said some things I shouldn't have said. But, in the end, I enrolled in Daddy's choice of college, lived at home four more years, and continued to be 'smothered' by my dad."

Dr. Kevin Leman calls this kind of parenting "overparenting." He writes: "The marks of overparenting are these. Instead of helping a daughter form her own opinions, an overparenting dad berates any idea that differs from his own. Instead of encouraging his daughter to become responsible, the overparenting dad encourages her to stay dependent. Instead of teaching his daughter to develop her strengths and abilities, an overparenting dad criticizes and coddles his daughter to such an extent she doesn't believe she has any strengths or abilities."[20]

A good friend of mine grew up with a father like Joyce's. Her dad's overparenting caused her similar problems.

"Dad wanted his kids to be good, law-abiding citizens," my friend admits. "He never encouraged us to try new things. He never seemed able to believe we could excel at anything that he himself hadn't done well at.

"Once I brought a piece of art to him that was pretty good. He expressed surprise and distrust that I'd actually done it myself. In looking back, I think that he was projecting his own insecurity and low self-esteem on me—how could his progeny do something artistic or different when he didn't see himself as capable of doing such? But it was discouraging to me. I felt I had to cross off from my list of choices anything related to art, and try just to be a practical contributor to society. I never felt my dad had confidence that I could strike out in something new and do well at it. I felt I needed to stay within the boundaries society draws in order to be safe."

My friend had the courage to spread her wings and fly on her own. She has discovered many remarkable hidden talents. But Joyce still remains sitting on her perch, not trying to spread her wings, not believing she can fly—not realizing that she has the potential to soar.

Joyce has never closely examined the freedom given to her by her heavenly Father. She sees God as an oppressive force that wants to manipulate her and keep her wings clipped. She has closed her heart to intimacy with her heavenly Father. "One smother-dad is enough!" she says.

A good father protects his daughter when she is young, but then teaches her how to operate her developing wings. When her wings are fully grown, he blesses her and allows her to fly.

I want to say to Joyce: "Examine your strengths, embrace your God-given freedom to make decisions and to take necessary risks. Gather up and throw away those wrong beliefs that keep you grounded and dependent on a father now deceased."

Did you grow up with a "smother-dad"? If so, allow me to tell you what I yearn to tell Joyce: "God, your heavenly Father, blesses you with the gift of freedom. You can learn to fly solo. You can soar." (On Day 3 of Week 4, you and Joyce will hear God's wonderful message: "God blesses you with freedom.")

Daily Sunlight

Your Personal Time to Grow:

Reread Ecclesiastes 3:11. Name five things that bring beauty to your life.

_____

_____

_____

_____

In light of Ecclesiastes 3:11, read John 3:16. How has God "set eternity" in your heart?

_____

_____

_____

What does this verse mean to you?

_____

_____

_____

_____

What freedom of choice does John 3:16 give you?

_____

_____

Have you ever felt like a "bird with clipped wings"? If so, describe this feeling. Where did it originate?

_____

_____

_____

Your Personal Prayer #1:

[Pray this prayer only if your father was like Joyce's father] My Savior, I have grown up with an overprotective, smothering father like Joyce's. I can understand Joyce's pain because I have experienced this same pain. Please uproot all the damage that my father's overparenting has caused me. I pray for my father. Please show me how to forgive him. In the name of your Son, amen.

Your Personal Prayer #2:

My heavenly Parent, I pray that all the Joyces in this world will experience the freedom you give to your daughters. Thank you for loving the world so much that you gave to it your only Son, Jesus. I pray that those lost people in the world will believe on Jesus and accept your priceless gift of saving grace. Thank you that you give them, and us, the choice to make. Help the world to turn to you, to depend on you, and to become those beloved gifted children you've created them to be. In Jesus' name, amen.

Week 2: A Time to Throw Away

Day 5: Amy's father, the dad who "just wasn't there"

> Daughters who have actively engaged fathers become more compassionate adults, have higher self-esteem, and form healthier relationships with men.
>
> Ken Canfield

When my seminary professor and friend, the late Dr. Wayne Oates, first coined the word "workaholic" with his book *Confessions of a Workaholic*, he could have been describing Amy's father. A self-employed workaholic, his work was his life, his religion, and his reason for getting up in the morning. When he wasn't traveling around the world, he spent fourteen hours a day at the office, six days a week. He liked fancy cars, impressive houses, and expensive clothes. He sent his three daughters to costly private schools. Amy and her sisters saw him for a few hours on Sunday during church, and afterward for lunch at their expensive country club.

"I can remember only one family vacation when I was a child," Amy reflects. "And then Daddy took his briefcase with him. He stayed in the resort room and worked while my mother and sisters and I played on the beach. Sometimes he wouldn't even stop to eat with us. We'd go to a nearby restaurant and dine alone. Daddy's work became his wife and children—his entire life. And he was just never there for us."

H. Norman Wright has a name for fathers who are uninvolved in their family's lives, and emotionally unattached from their daughters—"phantom fathers." He writes: "Some phantom fathers spend sufficient time in the home, but their interaction with their daughters is very superficial. This man may talk a little with his daughter about the news, work and sports, but he never reveals very much of himself.... They are emotionally detached from everyone."[21]

A phantom father resists an emotional nearness to his daughter, and she can feel invisible to him. He usually knows little about his daughter's hopes, dreams, and daily activities.

Amy's dad gave his girls lots of gifts, especially after a trip took him away for several weeks. "My childhood friends oohed and aahed over the dolls and bikes and party dresses I owned," Amy remembers. "But they couldn't have known how I envied them and their relationship with their dads. I often stood behind the drapes of my bedroom window and watched my friends help their dad barbecue on the grill, or wash the car, or rake the leaves. I could hear their laughter. Sometimes I joined in with my friends and their dads. But it just wasn't the same. I wanted my dad to be there for me. I wanted to help him do those things."

In her early teens, Amy tried to talk to her dad about his absence in her life. "We woke up early on Christmas morning, and my sisters and I dashed downstairs to open gifts. The beautifully wrapped, expensive gifts spilled from beneath the Christmas tree and covered the whole room. I knew that those boxes contained everything a girl my age could ever want or imagine. Yet I felt so empty. I tried to tell my father that I didn't want him to work so hard, that I could live without all those gifts, and that I would rather be with him. But he didn't hear me, and that made me so angry. He just didn't understand how lonely I felt, or how I craved his presence in my life."

Amy suffers from "father-hunger" caused by a dad who just wasn't there for her. "I felt like that deer in the Psalms that 'pants' and 'thirsts' for God," she cries. "The moment my Sunday school teacher read that verse to me as a child, I knew just how the deer felt (see Ps. 42:1–2). I missed my dad so much, it actually hurt me physically—inside and out."

As an adult, Amy admits she almost hates the name "father." "My definition of 'father' is a selfish, self-centered, materialistic workaholic who stays far, far away. I've often wondered: if a father truly loves his daughter, wouldn't he want to spend time with her? Wouldn't he care how she was feeling, what she was thinking, her ambitions, and her dreams?"

Amy, thirty-seven, has been married and divorced three times. Her extreme "father-hunger" entered into each marriage, and eventually ruined it. Everything her father failed to give her—attention, presence, affection—Amy demanded from her husbands. Amy emotionally suffocated each husband until he felt so weighed down by her overwhelming needs, he planned his escape. With each failed marriage, Amy's thirst for male attention, and her deep-rooted anger, increased. By the end of three divorces, Amy feels unlovable, rejected, sad, lonely, and bitter.

When viewed from outside Amy's expensive childhood home, one may have thought Amy had everything she possibly needed. She lacked for no material want. But her father neglected something far more important—her emotional needs, her need for his presence in her life. In doing so, Amy's father created deep-seated anger within her. The Bible calls it "provoking to wrath" (anger, rage, indignation) or "embittering" a child (see Col. 3:21). Scripture directs this message only to fathers: "Fathers, do not embitter your children, or they will become discouraged."

One way "to provoke your children to wrath is through neglect," writes John MacArthur in his book *What the Bible Says About Parenting*. "Fail to show them affection. Show them indifference instead. Don't take an interest in what interests them.... You will stir the wrath of your child."[22]

Unfortunately, as we see in Amy's life, "Our relationship with God is patterned after our relationship with our earthly father.... If your dad wasn't around much and didn't seem to care what you did so long as you kept out of his hair, you're going to believe that God isn't really all that interested in you either."[23]

Who is God to Amy? "I believe God is just like my dad—so busy running the universe that he has no time for anyone, especially me."

I yearn to tell Amy to stop and examine her false beliefs about God. I want Amy to take time to learn about God, to read his Word, to get to know him as Father—the one who surrounds her and indwells her with his constant attention and presence. The loving Father can help her release the anger and resentment that has built up inside of her. If she will let him, he can bring her into an "Abba" relationship with him. Until then, however, the volcano within her smokes, rages, and threatens to blow its top.

Perhaps you also grew up with an unloving father who just wasn't there for you when you so desperately needed him. Perhaps you carry anger in your heart and have allowed it to make you bitter and distant from God. Maybe you have much to "throw away" from a life spent with a workaholic father. Can you now find God's love and acceptance and presence in your adult life? Yes, you can! (On Day 4 of Week 4, we will see that "God promises you his constant presence.")

Daily Sunlight

Your Personal Time to Grow:

Read Ecclesiastes 4:1. Have you ever felt oppressed, and without a comforter? If so, please explain.

_____

_____

In Day 1, we discussed three biblical fathers—Lot, David, and Jacob—and witnessed how each failed his daughter in some crucial way. Each made his daughter feel comfortless. What surprised you about these dads? About their daughters? What characteristics would you change about each father?

_____

_____

_____

In Day 2 through Day 5, you met four women who also endured the poor character traits of human fathers: Alexandra, Bethany, Joyce, and Amy. Think about your dad for a moment. Did he, in any way, remind you of these fathers? If so, in what ways? Did they remind you of the fathers of any of your family members or friends? How?

_____

_____

_____

Last week we considered godly attributes that women most wanted their fathers to have. This week we'll look at negative character traits fathers can possess. When I asked a group of women to describe their dad's negative characteristics, their answers included the following:

Not disciplined physically, emotionally, mentally, or verbally	A poor listener	Avoids confrontation (even when necessary)
Doesn't easily communicate	Insensitive to family needs	Stubborn, immature, selfish
Spends too much; bad money manager	Not interested in self-education/ improvement	Not dependable
Watches too much TV	Dishonest and untrusting	Resents wife
Doesn't attend church; not a spiritual leader	Drinks/eats too much	Negative attitude
Finds fault with others; puts others down verbally	Doesn't care about people/ people's feelings	Workaholic
Controls and dominates	Hateful and irresponsible/ unloving and uncaring	Dishonors his parents
Doesn't help with housework or yardwork	Humiliates wife and children in front of others	Talks too much
Egocentric and arrogant	Doesn't forgive/holds grudges	Demands too much from others
Too strict	Uses silence to punish; withdrawn	Won't make commitments
Antisocial	Too dependent on wife or his mother	Lazy
Weak	Afraid to try new things	Addicted to power, drugs, alcohol, hobbies, sex, or pornography
Won't admit when he's wrong	Aloof	Defiant
Rebels against authority	Can't keep a job or won't work	Uses anger to manipulate/ intimidate others
Sarcastic, argumentative, obnoxious, or boring	Blames others for personal failures	Chronic joy-killer
Impatient	Favors one sibling over another	Self-absorbed, boastful

After reviewing this list, circle your father's top five ungodly personality/character traits that affected you as a child. Put an exclamation point beside your dad's top five negative traits that still affect you as an adult.

Last week, you envisioned your childhood as a garden where good plants grew. (While this might be considered an elementary exercise, it proves valuable in your journey toward healing.) This week, try to envision your childhood as a garden filled with hurtful plants—poison ivy plants that your parent planted there. As last week you named the good plants, take a moment now and name the bad plants. Describe how each plant made you feel as a child. (For example: "My father planted poison ivy in my childhood garden. Every time I touched it, I experienced rash and pain.") Now take a "look" at the garden of your adult life. What hurtful plants are still growing there? How do they make you feel? (For example: "My father planted stinging nettles in my garden. They still grow in my adult garden. They still hurt me whenever I touch them.")

_____

_____

_____

_____

If you choose to, find a box of crayons or colored pencils, and on a separate piece of plain paper draw a picture of your hurtful "garden" as it might have looked in your childhood, in your adolescence, and in your adulthood. (You need not show it to anyone. It is just for you.)

Name your human father's hurtful faults and ungodly personality/character traits that you want to "throw away" from your garden. Describe how each of his ungodly traits made you feel when he expressed them to you. (For example: "Whenever I most wanted to talk with my dad, he would never stop to listen to me. I felt unloved, unappreciated, and unimportant. I felt like he just didn't care about my life or feelings.")

_____

_____

_____

_____

List four truths you wished your father had taught you about God.

_____

_____

_____

_____

Write a brief letter to your human dad here—just a couple of sentences—or, if you'd like extra space, write it on a separate sheet of paper. (You don't have to mail it or show it to anyone.) Tell him all those things you most dislike(d) about him—those things you lived with that seemed harsh and unfair. Describe the occasions that could have been joyful and fun and meaningful (maybe a family trip or vacation or slumber party), but that his bad behavior or unkind words ruined for you.

_____

_____

_____

_____

Your Personal Prayer:

Dear God, please help me to trust you, to depend on your constant presence, and to know that you deeply love and accept me as your valuable daughter. Show me how you are my Comforter. Teach me that you are never "too busy" to hear me when I pray. Watch over me throughout my busy days, and guide me in all my decisions. In your Son's name, amen.

"A Time to Throw Away"

Growing Together in God's Word:

Over the past five days, we've examined the lives of many women who grew up with "flawed fathers." If you are comfortable doing so, briefly share how you might have experienced this in your own life as you answer the following questions:

1. In Ecclesiastes 4:2–3, Solomon makes some astounding statements. Read his words. Do you agree or disagree with him? Why? Name three things you most appreciate about life.

   _____

   _____

2. Have you ever known "conditional love" in your life? How did this type of love impact you and why? What kind of pain did it bring?

   _____

3. Read Colossians 3:18–21. What "rules" from this passage did your parents incorporate into your home life? How did they enrich your family life?

   _____

   _____

4. Amy admits she felt like the deer in Psalm 42:1. Read this verse. Have you ever felt like this? If so, please explain.

_____

5. Has your father ever "provoked" and "embittered" you, as Amy's father did? If so, how did his behavior impact you?

_____

6. How can a workaholic father produce feelings of anger, lack of love and acceptance, and bitterness in his children? Were either of your parents workaholics? If so, how did it affect you?

_____

7. Do you see God as Amy sees God: a busy Parent "so busy running the universe that he has no time for anyone," especially you? If so, explain.

_____

8. Did your parents give you both "wings" and "roots"? Describe how they each affected you.

_____

_____

Group Prayer:

[Pray this both silently and aloud together] My heavenly Parent, I feel sad when I think about my father's imperfection, his shortcomings, and his negative personality/character traits. I pray you will help me to understand my dad, and to forgive him. Keep me from ever holding a grudge against him, or feeling bitter. Guide me as I delve into the pain of my childhood, and as I seek to understand why I am now the way I am. I pray that you will help me to "throw away" my painful past, to forgive and pray for my flawed father. In Jesus' name, amen.

Week 3: A Time to Uproot

Day 1: Catherine's father, the abusive dad

> The sad truth is that home is where the greatest abuses in power and influence are committed against our most intimate relationships.
>
> Tim Kimmel, *Powerful Personalities*

Before we meet Catherine, let me tell you about two women who suffered extreme abuse from a father.

Aileen Wuornos, the infamous female serial killer, was the daughter of a child molester and sociopath who hanged himself in prison in 1969. Distraught and overwhelmed, Aileen's mother, Diane, abandoned her two small children. Aileen's maternal grandparents, Lauri and Britta Wuornos, adopted both Aileen and her brother, Keith. Unfortunately, life did not get better for Aileen. Her grandfather, Lauri, drank heavily and enforced brutal discipline. Aileen eventually rebelled against his severity, and became pregnant at age fourteen. The Wuornoses sent her to an unwed mothers' home, but by this time Aileen had become incorrigible. The staff found her hostile and uncooperative. Aileen stayed only until 1971, when she delivered an infant son. She put him up for adoption, dropped out of school, and took up hitchhiking and prostitution.

Aileen met and married an elderly man, Lewis Fell. Fell had a comfortable income. After a brief time, however, Fell had the marriage annulled. When he heard that police had arrested Aileen for assaulting a bartender, Fell obtained a restraining order. Her ex-husband accused Aileen of squandering his money and beating him with a cane. After the annulment, Aileen drifted in and out of trouble with the law. She met a twenty-four-year-old woman, Ty Moore, at a gay bar in 1986, and they become lovers. Aileen supported herself and Ty with her prostitution earnings. Aileen also began a killing spree throughout Florida that left seven men (strangers to her) shot dead. She now awaits execution on Florida's death row.[1]

Susan Smith also endured the abuses of two men in her early life—her birth father and her stepfather. Pregnant from a previous relationship, Susan's mother, Linda, just seventeen, married Harry Ray Vaughan, in 1960. An alcoholic, Harry violently abused Linda, and even threatened to kill her and himself. His behavior terrified young Susan and her brother, Scotty. In 1977, when Susan was six, Linda filed for divorce. Five weeks after the divorce became final, Harry broke into Linda's house. They argued violently, and Linda called the police. That night, Harry killed himself. His death devastated Susan. After Linda remarried, Susan, then sixteen, accused her stepfather of sexual abuse, but her mother pressured her not to press charges. Susan claimed the sexual abuse continued.

Before Susan's senior year of high school, she found a job at a local supermarket. After a brief time, she slept with an older married man, became pregnant, and had an abortion. After breaking up with another lover, Susan attempted suicide. She recovered and began dating her future husband, David Smith, who would become the father of her two children.

On the evening of October 25, 1994, Susan Smith, twenty-three, drove her car to a secluded boat ramp. Her two sons, Michael, three, and Alex, fourteen months, slept in the back seat. Consumed with loneliness, in the midst of divorce, and in love with a man who didn't want her children, Susan stepped from the car, put it in gear, and let it drift into the lake. She watched the car fill with water and submerge into the darkness, drowning her boys still strapped in infant seats. When the truth finally came out, Susan Smith's actions shocked a nation.[2] Like Aileen, Susan Smith—the abused, became Susan Smith—the abuser.

Catherine's name means "purity," yet her relationship with her father proved to be anything but pure. Catherine suffers from a deep sense of helplessness, hopelessness, and shame. She hates herself. She has few friends. She has no relationship with her heavenly Father. Why? Because Catherine's father abused her sexually, and she has never recovered from those deep wounds. The abuse started when Catherine was a preschooler. It continued throughout her adolescent years. Where was Catherine's mother, Margaret? She remained in the background, willfully closing her eyes to her daughter's abuse. She too suffered at his hands. Margaret had been so beaten down by her husband, she almost lost her mind.

At seventeen, Catherine ran away from home—she jumped out of the "frying pan" and directly into the "fire." She married a high school sweetheart who abused her even more than her father did. After several years, she divorced her abusive husband, but then fell into the arms of, and married, another spouse-abuser. She later divorced him too. When I talked with Catherine, she was a single mom, trying to raise a teenaged son. To her horror and regret, she had begun to see the same abusive character traits in her son that she saw in his father. She worried that he also would become a full-fledged abuser.

Let's talk for a moment about abuse. Abuse can take various forms: bruises, broken bones, and beatings; neglect; sexual molestation; name-calling; and so on. Abuse can come through neglect, as in the cases of Bethany and Amy. Abuse can come through harsh control, as in the situations of Alexandra, Joyce, and Aileen. In all its varied forms, abuse is ugly and life-damaging.

"Abuse is dangerous both mentally and physically. In its worst form it can bring death. In its most innocent form, it can kill a person's spirit and wound the soul to its deepest recesses."[3]

Catherine's father's steady sexual abuse killed her spirit. It set the stage for a lifetime of victimhood, first from her father, then from her two husbands.

"As a child," Catherine told me, "I always felt 'dirty.' I grew up feeling ashamed. My father—I can't even call him 'Dad'—violated me in horrifying, sexually perverted ways. I'd lie in bed and cry at night, afraid I'd hear his footsteps on the hardwood floor that led to my bedroom. When he crept into my room in the middle of the night, I vomited. As a preschooler, I'd scream out in terror for my mother. She'd never respond. His sexual abuse became so routine, I finally stopped calling out, crying, or vomiting. It didn't do any good anyway.

"During my junior year of high school, I planned my escape. I had been dating a boy I met in math class. He too had a hard time at home with a callous dad. We ran away, lived together for a while, and then, when I discovered I was pregnant, we married. I guess I should've known he would abuse me. When we were dating, he'd occasionally slap me or call me a terrible name. I shouldn't have married him, but I was pregnant and penniless. Not only did he hurt me, but he abused our infant son. That's when I left him. I found a job waitressing at a truck stop, and I became intimate with a regular customer, a driver who came in once a week for coffee. We ended up getting married, and he also turned out to be an abuser. After a few months of marriage, I 'escaped' from him too.

"How do I feel about men? I hate them. They make me feel dirty. I've spent most of my life taking hot showers, trying to scrub my skin clean. I worry that my son will become like my father, and his father.

"You ask me why I want no relationship with God? Because, according to Scripture, he carries the ugly name 'father.' I want nothing to do with him. And, I am sure, he wants nothing to do with me."

Catherine has lived her entire life in a state of humiliation and fear. Shame has been her constant companion. What is shame? Lewis B. Smedes describes shame as a "very heavy feeling," "a feeling that we do not measure up and maybe never will measure up to the sorts of persons we are meant to be." It's a "vague disgust with ourselves, which . . . feels like a hunk of lead on our hearts." Smedes also describes shame as a "lingering sorrow . . . an acute pain that stings you."[4]

Catherine feels shame, but not necessarily guilt. Smedes makes an interesting distinction between guilt and shame. He writes: "The difference between guilt and shame is very clear—in theory. We feel guilty for what we do. We feel shame for what we are. A person feels guilt because he did something wrong. A person feels shame because he is something wrong."[5]

"Guilt says, 'I've done something wrong'; shame says, 'There is something wrong with me.' Guilt says, 'I have made a mistake'; shame says, 'I am a mistake.' Guilt says, 'What I did wasn't good'; shame says, 'I am no good.'"[6]

The Difference between Guilt and Shame

GUILT SAYS:	SHAME SAYS:
"I've done something wrong."	"There is something wrong with me."
"I have made a mistake."	"I am a mistake."
"What I did wasn't good."	"I am no good."

Can Catherine find healing after being abused by a father and two husbands? Can Catherine dispel her negative ideas about God, and come to love and trust him as Father? Yes, she can!

What about you? Have you, like Catherine, been the victim of abuse? Do you suffer from shame? Do you need to find healing and cleansing for your soul? Know that you can find both in God. He can completely change your life. (On Day 1 of Week 5, we'll look at how God's love can cleanse you.)

Daily Sunlight

Your Personal Time to Grow:

In Ecclesiastes 4:5–6, Solomon describes the unhappy person who envies others. Have you ever envied someone? What feelings did it bring to your heart?

_____

_____

_____

Read John 4:1–42. (As you read these verses, mentally note the similarities between the Samaritan woman and Catherine.) Have you ever felt like the "Samaritan woman"? How? Have you ever felt like an outcast? Explain.

_____

_____

_____

Review the differences between guilt and shame in the chart on page 83. Recall two childhood experiences—one that made you feel guilty and one that made you feel shameful. How were your experiences of guilt and shame similar and dissimilar?

_____

_____

_____

_____

The legacy of abuse from Catherine's father led her to marry similarly abusive men and to raise a son who could potentially become an abusive father. Is there a legacy of abuse in your life? If so, what impact has it had on you and your relationships?

_____

_____

_____

Personal Prayer #1:

[Pray this prayer only if your father was like Catherine's father] Father, I have grown up with an abusive father like Catherine's father. I can understand Catherine's pain because I have experienced this same pain. Father, I pray that you will uproot all the damage that my father's abuse has caused me. I pray for my father, and I pray that you will show me how to forgive him for his crimes against me. In the name of your Son, amen.

Personal Prayer #2:

Father, I pray for all those girls and women, like Catherine, who deal with humiliating abuse. Whether physical, emotional, verbal, or sexual, you alone know how each one hurts, and the shame each one feels. Show these girls and women that you can heal their hurts and cleanse them from their shame. In Jesus' name, amen.

Day 2: Gayle's father, the critical dad

> An old Japanese saying lists the four most awful things on earth as: "fires, earthquakes, thunderbolts, and fathers." On my trips to Japan, many have told me of their authoritarian fathers who never apologize, who remain emotionally distant, who show nothing resembling love or grace, who offer much criticism and little if any encouragement.
>
> Philip Yancey, *Soul Survivor*

Kathleen Megan Folbigg's father, Thomas Britton (like Yancey's description of a Japanese father), displayed "nothing resembling love or grace." On a December evening in 1969, Britton stabbed his wife (Kathleen's mother) twenty-four times. Police arrested Britton, and he spent the next dozen years in prison. Kathleen, eighteen months old, stayed in an orphanage until, at age three, she was adopted. Not until she reached adulthood did Kathleen learn the awful truth about her father.

Kathleen married Craig Folbigg, and during a ten-year period, she gave birth to four infants. Shortly after the births, each infant died mysteriously. At first, the babies' deaths were attributed to natural causes, presumably Sudden Infant Death Syndrome. Later, however, police prosecutor Daniel Maher would tell the court "while each child's individual death had not raised much concern, their collective deaths could only be attributed to suffocation," and that "the circumstances surrounding the deaths were not consistent with Sudden Infant Death Syndrome or cot death." His examinations showed that "each child was found face up ... were still warm when found, and in two cases there were signs of life."

The truth finally came out when one day by accident, Craig discovered Kathleen's hidden diaries. He read how Kathleen had purposely killed each infant. In her diaries, Kathleen described the resentment she felt after each birth when her husband's attention shifted away from her to the new baby. She wrote about her "feeling of abandonment" just like she had experienced as a child—"in a family, but never felt like part of it." Another entry, made on October 14, 1996, after three of her children were already dead, includes these chilling words: "Obviously," she wrote, "I am my father's daughter."[7]

Gayle's father, Mike, also showed her nothing resembling love or grace. Instead he terrified her with his violent temper and "stabbed" her with his cutting criticism. He hatefully remarked about everything she said or did, and he used harsh punishment (or the threat of harsh punishment) to control her. He demanded perfection from her, and put high-voltage pressure on her to achieve and accomplish his own goals.

"Two events stand out most in my mind," Gayle remembers. "The first one happened on Valentine's Day when I was eight years old. Mother allowed me to have my first slumber party. I invited four of my favorite school friends to my home. Before they came, I cleaned my room and bathroom. I decorated my walls with colored-paper heart cutouts. Mother and I baked pink-iced cupcakes. My friends and I had eaten supper, and had gulped down a few cupcakes when I heard my father come in from work. He slammed the front door and cursed. I felt my stomach knot up. I didn't know why he was so angry, but I knew he would create some kind of bad scene. Some of my friends had left crumbs and empty cupcake papers on the kitchen counter. That set my father off. First, he yelled at me, and called me a 'pig.' 'Don't you know better than to leave trash all over the counter?' he shouted. Then, before I could apologize, he jerked me up by my arm and carried me to my bedroom. I remember staring at the little colored hearts on my wall as he whipped off his belt and beat me. I tried not to cry, but I couldn't keep quiet. When I returned to the kitchen, every one of my friends had called her mother and cried to come home. I never invited another friend to my house.

"The second embarrassment happened during our Thanksgiving dinner. I had returned home from college to spend the holiday with my mother and father, grandparents, uncles, aunts, and several cousins. We had just sat down at the beautifully set table, served our plates, and started to eat when my father jumped up from his chair. He stormed to my end of the table, and screamed: 'Gayle, don't you ever look at me like that again!' Then he took his large right hand and slapped me across the face. The force of his slap knocked me out of my chair and onto the floor. In total shock, and crying, I ran to my room. My family ate the entire dinner in stunned silence. I never quite understood what I had done to make my father so angry."

Gayle could do nothing right or good enough to please her dad. He criticized her without relief. Punishment included a belt beating, a slap, or an unkind criticism. For days after that, he ignored her. Instead of helping Gayle learn from her mistakes, he severely punished her, held his anger against her, and refused to ever talk about the incident again.

"Some parents seem to have the opinion that if discipline is good for a child, an abundance of discipline must be really good for them," writes John MacArthur. "They ride their kids constantly, holding the threat of corporal punishment over their heads like an unrelenting sword of Damocles. Such behavior is really nothing but brutality."[8]

It's interesting that MacArthur compares a father's threat of punishment to the sword of Damocles. The Roman orator, Cicero, told this story about the Greek tyrant Dionysius of Syracuse. Dionysius invited Damocles, his courtier, to a banquet. Above Damocles's head, by a single hair, the tyrant suspended a sharp sword. Throughout the dinner, Damocles ate in near-death suspense, not knowing when or if the hair would break and his head would roll.[9]

From under Dionysius's sword, Gayle grew up with low self-esteem and no self-confidence. As a grown woman, she still feels worthless. Even though her father died two years after Gayle finished college, she still "hears" her father's hateful voice criticizing her for everything she says or does.

"The low self esteem of many women is due in part to an ongoing tape recording of their father's critical voice playing over and over in their minds," writes Normajean Hinders.[10]

Gayle is afraid to take a risk or try anything new. She apologizes over and over to everyone for the smallest, most insignificant offense. Gayle strives for perfection, but she feels as if she will never quite measure up to her father's expectations. She is unsure of herself, restless, driven to accomplish, and never finishes anything she starts.

Gayle's view of God is as twisted and warped as her father's behavior. "When I think of God," she admits, "I see a stern, hateful Father who sits in heaven and watches for me to 'slip up' and make a mistake. He just waits to 'strike me dead.' I guess I'm as afraid of God as I was of my father. I greatly respect them both, but I don't want to have anything to do with either of them."

Gayle has some serious work to do. In order to heal, gain self-esteem, and build self-confidence, she must take a detailed look at the results of her father's criticism and brutality. She must study the attributes of her heavenly Father, and replace the ongoing tape recording of her father's critical voice with the voice of her heavenly Father—the voice that promises to love, accept, and discipline only with tenderness and grace.

Perhaps you also have grown up with a caustic, critical dad. Perhaps you've become a frustrated perfectionist, always striving to avoid your father's criticism, always fearful of failing. Your perfectionist tendencies can harm you. You must uproot them from your life and be rid of them.

"In order to prove that they are good enough, perfectionists strive to do the impossible," writes H. Norman Wright. "They set lofty goals and see no reason why they should not achieve them. But soon they are overwhelmed by the arduous task they have set for themselves. The standards of a perfectionist are so high no one could consistently attain them. They are beyond reach and beyond reason. The strain of reaching is continual, but the goals are impossible."[11]

If your childhood resembles Gayle's, know that you can find healing, hope, and total acceptance through your heavenly Father. (On Day 2 of Week 5, we'll see that "God totally accepts you.")

Daily Sunlight

Your Personal Time to Grow:

Read Ecclesiastes 4:7–12. Solomon describes the benefits of a companion or friend to journey with one throughout life. Bring to mind two or three of your closest friends. How do they help you as you journey throughout life, especially through hard situations? Do you agree that "a cord of three strands is not quickly broken"? If so, why? What does Solomon mean here?

Read Matthew 11:28–30. (As you read, notice how Jesus describes his "heart" and "yoke.") In your situation, what does this Scripture say to you?

Does Gayle's story in any way compare to your story? If so, in what ways?

_____

_____

_____

_____

Have you also known a father who criticized you, harshly punished you, and put pressure on you to be perfect? If so, how did it impact you—as a child? As an adult?

_____

_____

_____

_____

How did a critical father influence the way you now view God?

_____

_____

_____

_____

Your Personal Prayer #1:

[Pray this prayer only if your father was like Gayle's father] Father, I have grown up with a critical father like Gayle's father. I can understand her pain because I also have experienced this same pain. Father, I pray that you will uproot all the damage that my father's harsh criticism has caused me. I pray for my father, and I pray that you will show me how to forgive him. In the name of your Son, amen.

Your Personal Prayer #2:

Father, I thank you that my dad wasn't like Gayle's dad. My dad wasn't perfect, and he certainly had his faults, but I was spared from Gayle's trauma of criticism and pressure and harsh punishment. I love you, and I know that I am precious to you, as well as totally loved and accepted. In Jesus' name, amen.

Day 3: Faye's father, the undependable dad

> If your father was a weakling, and you couldn't depend on him to help
> you or defend you, your image of God may be that of a weakling. You
> may feel that you are unworthy of God's comfort and support, or that He
> is unable to help you.
>
> H. Norman Wright, *Always Daddy's Girl*

Born on July 13, 1950, Genene, an unwanted baby, was adopted by Dick and Gladys Jones. Genene lived with three other adopted children just outside San Antonio, Texas. Dick, a professional gambler and entrepreneur, operated nightclubs. But he was not a dependable wage-earner or dad. Working overtime, but living lavishly beyond his finances, he lost the business. A restaurant venture Dick attempted also failed.

When Genene was ten years old, police arrested Dick for burglary. The charges, however, were later dropped. Genene tried desperately to get attention from her busy parents. She felt unwanted, left out, lonely, and called herself the family's "black sheep." As Genene became older, she began to lie and to manipulate others. To get the attention she craved, she often pretended to be sick.

Two traumatic events happened in Genene's junior and senior years of high school. Her younger brother, Travis, made a pipe bomb that blew up in his face and killed him. And her father, at age fifty-six, refused medical treatment for cancer and died. The deaths devastated Genene. Her mother turned to alcohol to try to ease her pain. Genene graduated and married high-school dropout James DeLany Jr. They divorced several years later. Genene enrolled into beauty school, then decided to become a nurse. She worked as a licensed vocational nurse, but was fired from several hospitals before getting a job in the intensive care section of the pediatric unit of Bexar County Medical Center Hospital. That's where Genene's childhood caught up with her, and her life took a twisted, morbid turn.

Hungry for the excitement and attention she never had, Genene began to inject her child patients with heparin, a deadly drug. She created one medical emergency after the next, and thoroughly enjoyed the attention she received from confused doctors. By the time doctors caught on to her immoral tactics and the police arrested her, Genene had killed dozens of children on her afternoon "Death Shift." On February 15, 1984, a jury convicted Jones of murder. She received two sentences totaling 159 years—with the possibility of parole.[12]

Faye, like Genene, suffered under the weaknesses of an undependable dad. Faye couldn't count on him. His word meant nothing. He'd say one thing and then do another. She grew up hurt and confused by his broken promises. As a teenager, she finally figured out that if she wanted to survive, she'd have to depend on herself. She'd have to learn how to "pull herself up by her own bootstraps."

"I was always the last child to be picked up from school," she remembers. "Daddy said he'd be there at 3:00. I was usually still sitting on the playground at 5:00, waiting for him. Sometimes he never showed up.

"Daddy was kind and gentle with me and my brothers and sisters. We loved to go places with him, or just throw a baseball back and forth in the backyard. But he made promises he never kept. We'd be all dressed up and waiting for him to take us out for ice cream, and he'd never come. His word meant nothing to us."

As the oldest child of six brothers and sisters, Faye worried a lot about her mom's ability to keep a roof over the family's head. She also worried that her family wouldn't have enough to eat or receive adequate medical care. She started working at age fourteen to help out with family income. Every day after school, she waited tables at a nearby diner. She knew her mother had her hands full trying to make money and care for all her children.

"Daddy's undependability caused some major problems with my brothers. You see, Daddy wouldn't confront us or discipline us. He left the child rearing up to my mother. She did the best she could, but she couldn't control my delinquent brothers. One brother ended up in prison on an armed robbery charge. The other two became unsuccessful 'weaklings' like my dad."

Faye never made much of herself. She made poor grades in school. She had no ambition, and instead of going to college, she settled for a low-paying job after her high school graduation. She feels great insecurity—personal and financial. She feels unwanted and unloved.

Faye married a man as weak and undependable as her father—a common practice among women who suffered with weak fathers.

Ken Canfield explains: "As a girl tries to figure out what men are like, the first one she watches is her father. He can be one very significant example of a man who is consistent, trustworthy, and sensitive to feelings, who places his family at a high priority on his schedule, who keeps his promises, and who invests his energies in the lives of those around him. With such a positive reference point, she'll learn what to expect from the men she meets. You can bet she'll meet plenty of men who are dishonest, irresponsible, and chauvinistic, and she'll be able to see through them right from the start."[13]

Faye never learned to "see through" the men that drifted in and out of her life. She and her husband had several children, and, like her mother, Faye does most of the child rearing and discipline. To survive financially, she works full-time at minimum wage at a local supermarket. She can't depend on her husband to get up in the mornings and get to work. He's been fired from four jobs because he didn't show up, or came in late. "Every time he loses his job, we pack up and move to another part of the state," Faye says. "It's just like when I was a child. Sometimes my family moved in the middle of a school year. I always hated to start a new school mid-term. I decided early in life that it's better not to make friends than to have to keep leaving them. To this day, I have few friends."

Faye's mother contributed to her husband's weaknesses and lack of motivation. "Mom dumped on my dad continually. She treated him like a child. She continually told us kids he was a 'no-count,' 'good for nothing' human being. Like her, we had little respect for him."

How does Faye now view God? "To me he's a weak, inept Father that I don't dare depend on. Trust God? Never! I've been let down too many times to put my trust in anyone, even God. Anyway, I don't have time for God. It takes all my time and energy to work, take care of my kids, and just survive the day."

Faye never hurt or killed anyone like Genene did. But she also never bloomed in life. She has never reached a fraction of her God-given potential. Insecurity has kept her from growing and developing. She never lived in one place long enough to put down deep roots.

"When it comes to parenting, kids don't bloom and grow if their roots are constantly ripped out. Insecurity in a home pulls out roots; security provides the depth and shelter for them to thrive."[14]

Faye's father is like a gardener who plants seeds, and then ignores the garden. He doesn't stake and support the young seedlings, nor does he give them adequate water or fertilizer. He never prunes them. He just leaves them to grow on their own among thick, choking weeds.

In some ways, however, Faye was more fortunate than many girls today. Some daughters don't have a father in the home at all. Some have never even known a father. Single moms often struggle to raise emotionally healthy, secure daughters while they work full-time jobs and try to survive from day to day. They must be both mom and dad to their children.

"As a young girl and teenager," admits Faye, "I longed for a father who would provide me and my family with some kind of security. I wanted a dependable dad, a father who kept his promises, a dad who did what he said he'd do."

The time has come for Faye to discover, through deep Scripture study, that God the Father is dependable. Unlike her human father, he will meet her needs. God is all-powerful, and he always keeps his word.

"Faye," I'd like to say, "you can be so much more than you are. You need not allow your human father to influence your future for another day."

Can Faye come to know the Father who keeps his word, who helps her develop her full potential as his daughter? Yes, she can!

What about you? Do you still allow your human father to limit your God-given potential? Do you, like Faye, need to discover that God is all-powerful and dependable? You can! (On Day 3 of Week 5, we will see that "God always keeps his word.")

Daily Sunlight

Your Personal Time to Grow:

Read Ecclesiastes 4:13–5:3, in which Solomon gives some rich advice to the undependable people around him. How can his advice enrich your own life?

Read Psalm 139. What do verses 1–12 tell you about God's active involvement in your life?

_____

_____

What do verses 13–16 tell you about God's love and care for you?

_____

_____

Reread verses 23 and 24, and pray them as a prayer to God. Write that prayer in your own words here:

_____

_____

_____

Do you, like Faye, have some serious issues to work through relating to your dad's undependability? If so, list them.

_____

_____

_____

Because Faye's father failed to keep his word, the family was characterized by lack of trust, insufficient discipline, financial worries, and insecurity. What traits characterized your family because your father failed to keep his word?

_____

_____

_____

What did you learn from reading about Faye and her father? How does it help you in dealing with your own problems?

_____

_____

_____

Your Personal Prayer #1:

[Pray this prayer only if your father was like Faye's father] Father, I have grown up with an undependable dad like Faye's father. I can understand Faye's pain because I also have experienced this same pain. Father, I pray that you will uproot all the damage that my father's undependability has caused me. I pray for my father, and I pray that you will show me how to forgive him. In the name of your Son, amen.

Your Personal Prayer #2:

Father, I thank you that you are always dependable, and that I can trust you in all situations. You are always there for me, shaping, leading, and guiding my path. You care for me like you tend to the small birds of the air and the lilies of the field, and I am deeply appreciative. In Jesus' name, amen.

Week 3: A Time to Uproot

Day 4: Priscilla's father, the deadbeat dad

> Rejection communicates to you that you are not worth having a
> relationship with or even knowing. . . . True rejection means that you are
> not accepted at all and are treated as if you are a burden or millstone
> wrapped around your parents' or another person's neck. . . . We also tend
> to reject ourselves if we feel we were rejected by someone we care for.
> We treat ourselves like criminals and end up directing more criticism and
> disapproval toward ourselves than our parents or others ever gave us.
>
> H. Norman Wright, *Making Peace with Your Past*

Priscilla's dad, Fred, left his wife and children. He ate breakfast with his family, and then abandoned them. Vanished. They didn't know if he was dead or alive. He didn't file for divorce. He just left his family without a word. No explanation. No apology. No emotional support. No financial support. No medical insurance. Nothing. Gone without a trace. They never heard from him again. Fred became one of the world's many deadbeat dads.

The problem of deadbeat dads has become epidemic in our society. Some states have begun to aggressively search for and locate these irresponsible parents (also known as noncustodial parents) in order to establish or enforce a child support obligation and to collect unpaid child support from them.

Priscilla admits that she still loves her dad. And she misses him. They searched for him a whole year, and then accepted the fact that he was gone forever. "Even now, after all these years, every time the phone rings, I brace myself to hear news of him—a body found or a crime scene uncovered," Priscilla says.

She never recovered from her father's abandonment. As an adult, Priscilla harbors a deep disrespect for men in general. She doesn't trust them to fulfill promised obligations. She suffers from fear, insecurity, loneliness, and a lack of self-confidence and self-esteem. She also feels deep apprehension about her heavenly Father. She doesn't trust him either. She distrusts Scripture's declaration that God will never leave her or abandon her. She cries and thinks about her father's abandonment every day.

"My kids need [commitment and presence]—and so do yours," writes father Todd Wilson. "If we're not there for them, we handicap them and teach them that *God* isn't always there when they need Him. And I guess that makes the only force greater than *Father* Power—the power of a missing dad."[15]

Priscilla's insecurities, caused by a deadbeat dad, have wreaked havoc in her life and faith. As a teenager, she developed an eating disorder and experimented with sex, drugs, and alcohol. Two adolescent pregnancies ended in abortion. As an adult, she continues to battle obesity and depression. She still feels guilt and regret and self-loathing, and wonders if she might have caused her father's abandonment.

Lucy, like Priscilla, was abandoned by a deadbeat dad. But her story turned out quite different. Lucy explains:

"I saw it clearly as I scanned the obituary column in the morning newspaper. In bold print was my father's name. I hadn't seen him in years. I was only nine when he left our home. He and my mother divorced because of his unwillingness to provide for us. Even after he left, he refused to send any support for us. Early on, I learned what rejection meant.

"I read the short announcement again and was shocked to see that the only survivors listed were his third wife and one of my brothers. None of my other eight brothers and sisters, nor I, were listed. The feeling of rejection reared its ugly head again. Now I knew that I had never gained his love or acceptance, and never would. I wondered why he didn't want to claim us as his children. I thought back to the year I was fourteen, and remembered vividly a misfortunate meeting with him. My older brother and I had gone to a downtown coffee shop on Sunday night after church. As we stood in front of the glassed counter and placed our order, I noticed a well-dressed man come up to the counter next to my brother. Immediately my brother spoke to him. When I turned to look directly at him, I realized he was my daddy. He wasn't as handsome as I had remembered. He was noticeably balding and slightly stooped, but he still had a confident demeanor and was handsomely dressed.

"'Well, hello,' my brother said politely. 'I'm Tom. Do you remember me?'

"'Yes, I know who you are,' my daddy said, his anger quickly coloring his face. Moving restlessly from one foot to the other he looked at me and asked, 'Is that your girlfriend?'

"'No! No! That's Lucy. Don't you recognize her?'

"'Oh,' was his only reply as he turned abruptly to place his order with the waitress. Seeing that he didn't want any more conversation with us, we took our tray and walked over to find a table. We watched as he got his order and disappeared into the crowded restaurant. It must have been at that point I decided to forget him, to accept that he didn't want to have a relationship with me.

"Although I accepted Jesus Christ as my Savior when I was eleven years old, I knew nothing of the love of an earthly father and couldn't relate to God being my heavenly Father. It must have been four or five years after becoming a Christian that I finally began to understand and accept God's love for me. I had gone to talk to my pastor about a problem, and after counseling me, he said with all sincerity, 'I love you Lucy, just as I love my own daughter. That's how God's love is. He loves you as his own child.' This was the beginning of my journey of accepting his love.

"Even though I have never known the love of an earthly father, I have experienced over and over the love of my heavenly Father. The first time I read with understanding that I am his child, heir and joint heir with his son Jesus Christ (Rom. 8:17), I was overwhelmed. Each step of acceptance of his love led me to trust in his promises. He has supplied all my needs (Phil. 4:19). Indeed, I no longer feel rejected, for I know he will strengthen me and help me and uphold me with his righteous right hand (Isa. 41:10)."

Today Lucy is a wife, mother, and grandmother who deeply loves the Lord and actively ministers to everyone around her.

If you have suffered with a deadbeat dad, like Priscilla and Lucy, know that God offers you security within his eternal family. You are his daughter. He has forever committed his love to you. He promises never to leave you. Your life doesn't have to turn out like Priscilla's. You, like Lucy, can uproot those destructive lies your human father planted in your life. They need no longer control you. Unlike Lucy, Priscilla is still in pain. She hasn't yet discovered that God is dependable, keeps his word, and offers her eternal security. But God isn't finished wooing Priscilla. God has a great purpose for her, and he is presently and actively working in her life.

Unlike Priscilla's and Lucy's fathers, "God did not create the world and then just go away and leave it. Moment by moment He is sustaining and governing this universe in which we live . . . He is actively at work directing everything and causing all events to ultimately fulfill His great purpose."[16]

Can Priscilla learn that God is the committed Father who will never leave her? Can she uproot those lies planted deep within her heart and mind? Can she find a love and trust for her heavenly Father that will fill the emptiness in her heart? Yes, I believe she can.

And so can you. If you grew up with a deadbeat dad, you can know the security of a Father who holds you in the palm of his hand. Forever. (On Day 4 of Week 5, you and Priscilla will learn that "God will never leave you.")

Daily Sunlight

Your Personal Time to Grow:

Read Ecclesiastes 5:4–7. Describe your sense of "awe" when you "stand" before God.

_____

_____

In Romans 8:16–17, the apostle Paul writes that the Spirit himself testifies with our spirit that we are God's children. In Philippians 4:19, Paul also affirms that God will meet all our needs according to his glorious riches in Christ Jesus. How do these promises impact your view of God as a Father? How does each Scripture encourage you?

_____

_____

_____

_____

Being abandoned by her dad produced feelings of deep insecurity in Priscilla. If you experienced abandonment by your father, how did it impact you?

_____

_____

_____

Because of her dad's leaving, Priscilla felt rejected and unloved by God. How did your father's behavior influence how you feel about your relationship with God?

_____

_____

_____

_____

What have you learned from Priscilla's and Lucy's stories?

_____

_____

_____

Your Personal Prayer #1:

[Pray this prayer only if your father was like Priscilla's father] Father, I have grown up with a deadbeat dad as did Priscilla and Lucy. I can understand their pain because I also have experienced it. Father, I pray that you will uproot all the damage that my deadbeat dad has caused me. I pray for my dad, and I pray that you will show me how to forgive him. In Jesus' name, amen.

Your Personal Prayer #2:

Father, I understand that you love me, and that I, as your daughter, am secure in your eternal family. But I pray today for the many women and girls who are in need physically, emotionally, and spiritually because of the pain of abandonment. Come alongside them and, as I have opportunity, may I come alongside as well. In Jesus' name, amen.

Day 5: Karen's father, the addicted dad

> God is a Spirit, infinite, eternal, and *unchangeable* in his being, wisdom, power, holiness, justice, goodness and truth.
>
> Westminster Shorter Catechism, my emphasis

Drug- and alcohol-addicted dads often influence their daughters to become drug and alcohol addicts too. Consider three actresses who were influenced to drug dependencies through family ties: Drew Barrymore, MacKenzie Phillips, and Kelly Osbourne.

Drew Barrymore is the daughter and granddaughter of famous, and hard-drinking actors John Barrymore and John Drew Barrymore Jr. At age eight, Drew became involved with drugs and alcohol. She lived a troubled early life, undergoing drug rehab for a cocaine addiction, and attempting suicide in July 1989. At age fifteen, Drew legally divorced her mother. She had little or no relationship with her absentee father.[17]

MacKenzie Phillips, best known for her acting roles in the film *American Graffiti* and on television's *One Day at a Time*, was the daughter of drug-addicted John Phillips, a '60s pop star and member of the singing group "The Mamas and the Papas." MacKenzie admits her drug addiction was "encouraged by growing up in a home where drugs were prevalent." She often "got high" with her father, who used heroin, cocaine, amphetamines, and alcohol. By age fifteen, MacKenzie had become a full-fledged drug addict. Now a mother herself, she has struggled most of her life trying to overcome her drug addictions.[18]

Kelly Osbourne, nineteen-year-old daughter of talk show host Sharon Osbourne and Black Sabbath's former front man Ozzy Osbourne, has recently undergone drug rehab. Kelly followed in the footsteps of her famous drug-addicted father, Ozzy, a rumored psychopath and Satanist whose heavy metal concerts included biting off a live bat's head and other "spectacles of gore." Kelly tried alcohol at twelve, and then used hard drugs.

She admitted recently: "There wasn't a second in a twenty-four-hour day that I wasn't high on something." She too attempted suicide. Her brother, Jack, also has been treated for drug addiction.[19]

Children pay close attention to the good and bad habits of their parents. As young girls, Drew, MacKenzie, and Kelly watched their fathers develop and feed an addiction. Drugs and/or alcohol became a normal part of daily life in their dysfunctional homes.[20] Looking up to their fathers as their trusted authority figures, these girls imitated their dads' bad habits and ended up wasting precious years trying to kick addiction miseries.

Karen's father had a drug and alcohol addiction. And he too passed his addiction to his daughter.

"My father spoke softly and was kind and loving when he wasn't high on drugs or drunk on alcohol," Karen remembers. "But when he was high or drunk, watch out! He turned violent. He'd throw furniture, shout obscenities, call us horrible names, and sometimes threaten us physically.

"He'd also embarrass us in front of our friends. I never invited school friends over because I didn't know if Dad would come home drunk or sober. My muscles tensed when I heard his car drive up. My mother and I waited anxiously each afternoon to see how he walked through the front door.

"One day Dad showed up at my school to drive me home. That was unusual. Usually Mom picked me up or I rode the bus. My teacher took a sniff of Dad's liquored breath. Then she watched him weave as he tried to walk across the school hallway. She confronted Dad with his drunkenness, and she wouldn't let me go with him. My dad became violent with my teacher, and he even threatened her. That's when she called the police, and they arrested Dad. All my school friends watched as the officers handcuffed him and put him in the police car. I have never been so embarrassed in my life.

"Dad's arrest prompted my mother to divorce him. The divorce proved a bitter battle, one that left scars on both my mother and me."

Even though Karen had a deep distaste for her father's habits, she still developed his addictions. And like Drew, MacKenzie, and Kelly, she spent valuable time and money trying to find a cure.

Karen's mother, a devout Christian woman, tried in vain to bring Karen to a true understanding of her trustworthy heavenly Father. But Karen viewed God as she saw her birth father: wishy-washy, untrustworthy, a father so wrapped up in himself that he didn't have time to love and care for his hurting daughter.

Fathers who allow addictions to rule their lives are selfish fathers. Addictions to drugs and alcohol can cause a father's temperament to change quickly—from Dr. Jekyll to Mr. Hyde with no warning. They can often terrify young daughters. Fathers with addictions to sex and pornography, and even to work and hobbies, can put up an impenetrable barrier that separates them from their families and eats away time that could be spent together. Fathers with addictions need help. Many programs exist today to help addicted parents overcome their addictions and once again become trustworthy and available to their families.

Can Karen ever learn to trust her heavenly Father even though she found her human father untrustworthy? Yes, she can! She will have much work to do. First, she must uproot those lies planted deep within her heart and mind by a drug-addicted dad. Trust will, no doubt, come slowly for Karen, but it can come. She can find a deep, trusting relationship with the Father in heaven who dearly loves her.

If you've been the victim of a dad who struggles with addiction, you also can find intimacy with your heavenly Father. Examine the attributes of God, and seek to trust him. He will change your life. (On Day 5 of Week 5, we will see that "God never changes; he is totally trustworthy.")

Daily Sunlight

Your Personal Time to Grow:

Read Ecclesiastes 5:8–20. Have you ever known the "frustration, affliction, and anger" Solomon speaks of? Did your father cause any of it? If so, describe the situation. Did you find resolution? How?

Review the list you made last week when you named your father's faults and flaws. During this exercise, write down the results of your father's failures. What have been the lasting results that have followed you into adulthood? In what areas of your life have you suffered because of his failures? What bad decisions have you made that come directly as a result of your father's character/personality flaws? (For example: "Since my father sexually abused me, I learned to hate all men in general." "My father's constant harsh criticism of everything I did made me grow up with no confidence in my ability to do anything worthwhile." "My father's tendency to 'smother' me, and to overparent me, made me reluctant, and almost unable, to make decisions on my own as an adult.")

_____

_____

_____

_____

_____

_____

_____

Now, on a separate sheet of paper, write a letter to your father and tell him how his faulty fathering followed you into adulthood. (Don't send the letter. It will be used only by you as a healing tool.) Tell him exactly how his negative character traits and treatment of you as a child makes you now feel as an adult. (For example: "Dad, your sexual abuse still makes me feel great shame. I don't trust men and their motives. Your abuse has affected my sexual relationship with my husband. I must admit I hate you for what you did, for your deceit, and for your selfish abuse." Or, "Dad, as a child, I never felt like I could please you no matter how hard I tried. You always seemed to correct or criticize everything I did. Now, as a grown woman, I try too hard to please people, and I feel sad and act defensively when anyone criticizes me, even if the criticism is constructive and helps me.")

Spend some quiet time in prayer as you reflect on your father and the results of his failures toward you. Pray that God will bring to mind everything he wants you to deal with today. (No doubt, this exercise will be painful for you, but it is necessary for understanding and uprooting.)

(This next exercise is a powerful one. If you need to defer it until you feel more ready, please do so. Or, you might want to consider doing it under the guidance of a trained psychotherapist, pastoral counselor, or wise friend.) Go to a quiet place where you won't be interrupted. Place two chairs facing one another. Sit down in one chair with the information you just wrote. Imagine your human father sitting across from you. As you "see" him in your mind's eye, notice what he is wearing, how he is looking at you, his body language—the way he is sitting or slouching or frowning, whatever. Sit quietly until you can capture his image and until you feel comfortable.

When you are ready, "look" him in the eye and talk to him. Tell him everything you wrote down on your lists (from last week and this week). If you need to shout, then shout. If you need to cry, then cry. Take as much time as you need. Tell him all the ways he hurt you as a child. Tell him all the ways he has hurt you as an adult. Leave nothing out. Tell him exactly how you are feeling at this very moment. (For example: "Daddy, I feel so angry right now. I feel as if I'll never recover from the sexual abuse you inflicted upon me. I feel like I want to hate you forever for what you put me through.")

After you have said everything you want/need to say to your imaginary father, then tell him one more thing. In your own words, tell him what you are going to do with all the "harmful, poisonous plants" he has "planted" in your "life-garden" from your childhood to the present. (It might sound something like this: "Daddy, I am no longer going to allow the poison you planted in my childhood and adolescent garden to grow there. Your poison has no place in my life now. I am an adult woman. God's Word tells me that the 'truth' will set me 'free' [John 8:31–32]. I have yearned for years to be free from your _____ [list your father's abuses]. Though I will honor you as my father—as Scripture tells me to do—I will not continue to allow you to influence and control my life in bad ways.")

The next step you take depends on you. Here are some suggestions to help you.

Tear into little pieces and throw away the picture of your garden you drew last week. Allow this action to represent uprooting and throwing away your childhood hurts caused by an unkind father. (Some women choose to burn the picture. If you decide to do this, be sure you are in an open place and use proper fire safety measures.)

Envision yourself walking through your garden. Imagine that, one by one, you bend down, grasp the poisonous plant by the roots, and pull it up. Then imagine that you are throwing the uprooted plant into a fire and destroying it. Continue to uproot the bad plants until they all are completely destroyed. Then imagine you are walking through your cleared garden. It is bare. The bad plants are gone, roots and stems. The empty garden soil waits in the sunlight for you to plant new, healthy plants where the bad plants once grew.

On a new sheet of plain paper, draw a picture of your cleared garden. Pencil in the deep holes where bad plants once grew—the plants you uprooted and destroyed.

Now imagine that your father has stood up and left the room. Sit quietly and think about what you have just done and accomplished.

You have confronted your father (in an imaginary scene), and you have expressed your feelings, your anger, and your future intentions.

You have chosen the harmful plants your father planted in the garden of your childhood, and you have decided they should not be growing in your adult garden any longer.

You have reached down deep, and you have uprooted the harmful plants. You pulled them up completely by the roots so that they will not grow there again.

You have destroyed the poisonous plants forever.

You have imagined your new garden, now cleared and waiting for you to choose and plant new healing herbs that will grow and thrive in its rich soil.

Your Personal Prayer #1:

[Pray only if you have completed the suggested exercises] Father, this exercise has drained me. It took time and energy. It proved painful as I delved into the sore spots and hurtful memories of my childhood with my father. But, I see that this exercise was necessary. I am glad to finally be free of my father's bad influences that have plagued my childhood and adulthood. I have chosen to rid my garden of its poisonous plants. They are gone. Destroyed. I will never allow them to grow again in my garden. Father, I am now left with bare ground. Nothing grows in my new garden. I yearn to till the soil and plant healing herbs where the poison ivy once grew. Show me how to prepare the soil for my new plants. I am eager to begin my gardening and my planting. In the name of your Son, amen.

Your Personal Prayer #2:

[Pray this prayer if you have not yet begun or completed the suggested exercises] My dear Savior, I understand that these exercises are part of a longer process. I don't feel quite ready to engage in these steps now. I pray that when I do feel ready to start them and complete them, you will enter into this course of action with me. I long to be free of my father's negative influences that have caused me such pain for so long. In your name, amen.

"A Time to Uproot"

Growing Together in God's Word:

1. Read Ecclesiastes 3:2. Discuss together what Solomon means by "uprooting" in this verse. Have you known "uprooting" in your life? If so, explain.

   _____

   _____

   _____

2. Name the problems Drew Barrymore, MacKenzie Phillips, Kelly Osbourne, and Karen shared in common. Can you identify with any of these women? If so, in what ways?

   _____

   _____

3. Have you ever had a problem, or have known someone close to you who had a problem, with addictions? If so, and only if you are comfortable, please explain.

   _____

   _____

   _____

4. Do/did you find it hard to trust your father? Why?

_____

5. Read aloud in unison Psalm 34:17–18. This passage describes God's promises to be close to the brokenhearted and to save those who are crushed in spirit. Have you experienced God's closeness to you in your brokenness over your father? If so, how? If not, how might you begin to allow God into this area of your life?

_____

_____

_____

6. Read Hebrews 13:6 and Deuteronomy 31:6. What have you learned from Scripture about God's presence in your life? In light of this promise, how should you live your life?

_____

_____

_____

7. What good traits of your heavenly Father do you most want to plant in your garden right now?

_____

_____

_____

Group Prayer:

Father, please give special attention to those daughters who must deal with drug- and alcohol-addicted dads. Give them the needed strength to deal with the problems that addictions inevitably bring into a family. Keep us free from those things that would harm us. And keep us centered always in your Word and in your will. In Jesus' name, amen.

Your Heavenly Father

During Weeks 2 and 3, you met hurting women who suffered under seriously flawed fathers. Alexandra's father was a harsh controller; Bethany's dad was distant and unapproachable; Joyce's dad over-parented and smothered her; Amy's father just wasn't there for her; Catherine's father sexually abused her; Gayle's father criticized her; Faye's dad was undependable; Priscilla's dad abandoned her; and Karen's father influenced her into a life of addictions. We discovered three fascinating facts about the father-daughter relationship:

1. Flawed fathers can leave a daughter with lasting pain that she may never stop to examine.
2. Flawed fathers can influence a woman's entire lifetime.
3. Flawed fathers can color how a woman views God.

During Weeks 4 and 5, I want to personally write a letter to each woman about her heavenly Father, telling her how she can embrace his love, and how she can plant his fruit-producing plants in all the places where poison ivy once grew. I also want to suggest a healing herb—one used in biblical days—that each woman can plant and use for healing.

These letters are also written to you—hurting women who have suffered under flawed fathers. They are also intended for those hurting women you know—in your family, your neighborhood, your church, your school, your work, and your world—who need to hear God loves them as their perfect Father. The words in these letters come directly from God's Word as he expresses his love for you and to you.

During the next two weeks, we will consider the new gardening tasks that lay ahead for you. In Week 4 we will study an assortment of healing plants—plants that represent the wonderful attributes of God, your heavenly Father. These are the plants that will grow and thrive and produce fruit in your new garden. These are the plants that will encourage, strengthen, and sustain you for the rest of your life.

Week 4: A Time to Trust, A Time to Embrace

Day 1: Alexandra, God loves you unconditionally

> Love is the definition of God. It is His essence. It is what makes God God.
>
> Joseph F. Girzone, *Never Alone*

On Day 2 of Week 2, I introduced you to Alexandra, a woman who suffered throughout her childhood and adolescence under the domination of a controlling, harsh, unloving father. (Please take a moment and briefly review her story.) Here is my letter to Alexandra.

Dear Alexandra:

Please allow me to introduce you to your true Father—your Father in heaven. He is nothing like your human father. I know you "can't go back and give yourself a new earthly father, but you can find the comfort, love, and affirmation you crave from your daddy by looking heavenward and getting to know your spiritual Father."[1]

With your heavenly Father, you no longer need to fear harsh punishment, nor must you fear failure. You can uproot those harmful perfectionistic hang-ups imposed by a flaw-picking father. You can look to your heavenly Father who loves you without condition, and in spite of your inevitable mistakes and failures. You don't have to perform for God like a masked actress on a stage. God knows that human beings can fall and stumble. He loves, and he forgives; he helps you back to your feet and gives you another chance. You need no longer become like Jello forming to society's mold. You can be transformed into God's mold. "Do not conform any longer to the pattern of this world, but be transformed by the renewing of your mind. Then you will be able to test and approve what God's will is—his good, pleasing and perfect will," Paul writes (Rom. 12:2). You can find the freedom to be, and to become, the woman God created you to be.

Through God's Holy Word, let me show you the unconditional love of your heavenly Father.

Nothing can separate you from God's love ... not "trouble or hardship or persecution or famine or nakedness or danger or sword.... No, in all these things we are more than conquerors through him who loved us." Nothing in all creation "will be able to separate us from the love of God that is in Christ Jesus our Lord" (Rom. 8:35, 37–39). God loves you with a love that lasts forever, a love that nothing can sever.

Jesus said: "As the Father has loved me, so have I loved you. Now remain in my love.... Greater love has no one than this, that he lay down his life for his friends" (John 15:9, 13.) Jesus laid down his life for you because he loves you. He wants to be your best friend.

God's love is filled with mercy and grace. Grace is a free gift. You don't need to earn it. "But because of his great love for us, God, who is rich in mercy, made us alive with Christ even when we were dead in transgressions—it is by grace you have been saved" (Eph. 2:4). Nor is grace anything you can achieve by a perfect performance. "For it is by grace you have been saved, through faith—and this not from yourselves, it is the gift of God—not by works, so that no one can boast" (vv. 8–9).

God is not a flaw-picking father like your dad. God loves you in spite of your weaknesses. He shows great compassion when you stumble. God "knows how we are formed, he remembers that we are dust" (Ps. 103:14).

God loves you with a perfect love. You can "know and rely on the love God has for" you. For "God is love," and "there is no fear in love.... perfect love drives out fear ... we love because he first loved us" (1 John 4:16, 18–19).

Unlike your human father, God "does not act like a military commander; he treats us like a gracious Father. God doesn't set a legalistic standard; he sets a holy standard." What is the difference? "Legalism stands harsh, strict, and unbending. Holiness recognizes weaknesses, deals with sin, and works for growth. Legalism seeks to crush people with the standard. Holiness seeks to call people to the standard."[2] God gives tender guidance with a gentle hand that leads you with his love. And that love and grace is unconditional.

Uproot those unproductive plants that were put into your garden soil long ago by a flawed father. Trust your true Father, the one who accepts you. Expect his gift of grace. Know that "grace is the beginning of our healing because it offers the one thing we need most: to be accepted without regard to whether we are acceptable. Grace ... is the gift of being accepted before we become acceptable."[3]

God's love surrounds you. The love of his Son, Jesus Christ, walks beside you. The love of his Holy Spirit lives within you. "I have written your name on my hand," claims our loving God (Isa. 49:16).

In closing, allow me to leave you with a quote from a favorite writer, Charles Stanley. "It takes a long time to get over being in a relationship with a person who gives conditional love," he writes, "especially if that person is a parent or a spouse. A person who has lived for years with someone who loved him or her conditionally nearly always is suspicious of the phrase 'I love you.' In one way or another, that person tends to ask, 'Why?' He or she wants to know what the other person is expecting, why the individual is saying 'I love you,' and what it is that the person wants in order that that loving feeling be sustained . . . the person who is accustomed to conditional love is a person who can never fully relax in a relationship. There's always the potential for making a mistake, missing a cue, or disappointing someone in some way. The result is tension and an abiding anxiety."[4]

You have no reason to be suspicious of the phrase "I love you" that God pronounces clearly throughout his Word. You can fully relax in your relationship with God, your true Father. Whether you make a mistake, miss a cue, or disappoint him in some way, you need not feel tension and anxiety. God is love—absolute love without limitation—and you can rest in that love forever.

Daily Sunlight

Your Personal Time to Grow:

What does Solomon write about wisdom in Ecclesiastes 7:11–12? Do you agree with him? What role has wisdom played in your life? In the lives of your parents, siblings, grandparents, etc.?

_____

_____

_____

_____

Read Romans 5:8; Ephesians 2:8–9; and 1 John 4:9–10, 16, 18–19. What do these verses tell you about God's love?

_____

_____

_____

_____

Joseph Girzone writes: "Love is the definition of God. It is His essence. It is what makes God God." If you agree with Girzone, in what ways have you felt God's love in your life?

_____

_____

_____

_____

Name three of God's perfect attributes that you need to commit to believing, and why.

_____

_____

In your opinion, what is meant by God's words: "I have written your name on my hand" (Isa. 49:16)? What does this scriptural statement mean to you?

_____

_____

_____

_____

If I could suggest an herb for you to plant in your new garden, it would be *saffron*. Many believe that saffron was used as early as prehistoric Greek times. During biblical times, saffron was the world's most expensive spice. It took 4,300 saffron flowers to make just one ounce; 75,000 flowers to make one pound. Used for dying clothes, as an expensive perfume, and for gastric problems, saffron—because of its preciousness, rarity, and value—is a wonderful symbol of God's unconditional, precious, and rare love.

Your Personal Prayer:

Father, in your Word you tell me that I am saved by grace through faith, that I cannot earn grace, but that grace is a free gift to me through your Son, Jesus. Thank you, Father, for your priceless gift of eternal life, a gift as rare and precious as saffron. Help me never to forget what my eternal salvation cost Jesus. I pray that I might always receive the love and grace you so freely offer. In the name of your Son, amen.

Week 4: A Time to Trust, A Time to Embrace

Day 2: Bethany, God is kind, compassionate, and approachable

> One of the greatest gifts a father can present to his daughter is to be approachable. Approachability involves communication at a level where your dad is open, non-defensive, interested and responsive. Approachability requires tenderness and sensitivity to hurt or feelings of insecurity. It means being a companion. Approachable fathers listen carefully to what a daughter may have difficulty verbalizing. He listens not only with his ears, but with his eyes and his heart as well.
>
> H. Norman Wright, *Always Daddy's Girl*

On Day 3 of Week 2, I introduced you to Bethany, a woman who suffered under a "chronically AWOL dad"—a father whose heart was wrapped in concrete, and who ignored his daughter emotionally. (Please take a moment and briefly review her story.) Here is my letter to Bethany.

Dear Bethany:

God, your true Father, bestows love that covers you with kindness. I learned about kindness from my own father—a gentle, kind, and caring man. God is also approachable, only a prayer away from you at all times. Through God's Word, let me show you God's incredible kindness and compassion.

Titus 3:4–5	It was with the "kindness and love of God [that] our Savior appeared . . . he saved us, not because of righteous things we had done, but because of his mercy."
Mark 6:33–44	It was with compassion and kindness that Jesus fed five thousand hungry people.
Luke 7:11–17	With compassion and kindness, Jesus reached out to the widow at Nain during her only son's funeral procession. "When the Lord saw her, his heart went out to her and he said, 'Don't cry.'" Then he touched the dead boy and raised him to life and gave him back to his mother.

God is always accessible, open, and easy to talk to.

You can approach him. Jesus constantly extended his hands to the hurting, the helpless, and the hopeless. "Come to me," Jesus invites, "all you who are weary and burdened, and I will give you rest" (Matt. 11:28).

You can seek him. Jesus invites us to "ask and it will be given to you; seek and you will find; knock and the door will be opened to you. For everyone who asks receives; he who seeks finds; and to him who knocks, the door will be opened" (7:7–8).

You can trust him. God welcomes us to ask him directly for those things we need. "Which of you," he asks, "if his son asks for bread, will give him a stone? Or if he asks for a fish, will give him a snake? If you, then, though you are evil, know how to give good gifts to your children, how much more will your Father in heaven give good gifts to those who ask him!" (vv. 9–11).

You can talk with him. People felt comfortable coming to Jesus. Consider: The man with leprosy who came down from the mountainside and knelt before Jesus and said, "Lord, if you are willing, you can make me clean" (8:1–2).

Scripture is filled with people who freely approached Jesus and asked for his help.

God makes himself approachable to his children through his gift of prayer. Jesus teaches us to pray to "our Father" (Luke 11:2). He teaches us to pray with boldness and persistence, like the widow in Luke 18:1–8. He shows us the power and passion of prayer when he himself prays intimately with God the Father (Matt. 26:39, 42; Mark 1:35; Luke 22:39–46; John 11:41–42; 17:1–26). Paul continues Jesus' teachings on prayer. He writes: "Pray continually" (1 Thess. 5:17); "Devote yourselves to prayer . . . and pray for us, too" (Col. 4:2–3).

Jesus also wishes to be your friend. And he wants to be an easily approachable friend. He tells you in Scripture, "I am the vine; you are the branches" (John 15:5). "If you remain in me and my words remain in you," Jesus promises, "ask whatever you wish, and it will be given you." He shares himself with you (vv. 13–15). He invites you to also share yourself with him.

God the Father could have chosen to rule us with distant and indifferent authority in a cold, insensitive manner. He could have been a heavenly Father with fangs. Instead, he chose to be a tender, compassionate, kind, and loving nurturer. Surely, he has "loved you with an everlasting love" and he has "drawn you with loving-kindness" (Jer. 31:3).

Only God the Father can fill the father-hunger hole in your heart. Reconnect with him for "your father hunger is actually a longing to reconnect with the God who made you, your spiritual Father in heaven."[5]

Daily Sunlight

Your Personal Time to Grow:

Read Ecclesiastes 7:14. Name what is currently "good" in your life. Describe what Solomon says about "bad" times. What is currently "bad" in your life?

_____

_____

_____

_____

Read Matthew 8:1–2. The leper made a request of Jesus. What request do you most want to make of Jesus right now?

_____

_____

_____

Read Matthew 19:13–14: Little children seemed deeply drawn to Jesus. He always welcomed them into his arms. Are you drawn to Jesus? If so, how do you want Jesus to welcome you? If not, why do you think that is the case and what would need to happen to change the situation?

_____

_____

_____

_____

I believe *lavender* is the herb that best represents God's kind approachability. A delicate flowering herb known for its sweet, soothing scent, lavender, like God's kindness and compassion, gently draws one to itself. Lavender grows soft, beautiful, violet-colored flowers whose oils are used in many perfumes. I suggest that you plant lavender in your new garden, and that you allow its fragrance to draw you into its soothing peace.

Your Personal Prayer:

Father, I thank you that I can approach you without fear, that I can rejoice in your kindness and rest in your compassion. Help me to experience the drawing power of your love—an approachable Father whose gentle fragrance, like lavender, invites me to come to you. Please fill the father-hungry hole in my starving heart. In Jesus' name, amen.

Week 4: A Time to Trust, A Time to Embrace

Day 3: Joyce, God blesses you with freedom

> All of our children are unique gifts from God. We need to cherish each child with obvious love and affection, recognizing each child's unique personality, individual capabilities, and special needs.
>
> Alistair Begg, *The Hand of God*

On Day 4 of Week 2, I introduced you to Joyce, a woman who suffered under a dad who made all her decisions, wouldn't let her grow up and become independent, and refused to bless her and give her freedom. (Please take a moment and briefly review her story.) Here is my letter to Joyce.

Dear Joyce:

Your ultimate Father—your Father in heaven—will never expect you to be "like a seal that claps its flippers when Daddy holds out a fishy little morsel." God encourages you to fully grow and expand your wings and fly. He gives you his blessings and allows you to make your own decisions. He is in no way a "smother-dad."

God encourages his daughters to think. Jesus taught theology to the women who followed him during his ministry, as well as to the men. God has given us, his daughters, his Holy Word as a guidebook to instruct us, to teach us how to become responsible, to help us make our own decisions. He could have created us as robots. Instead he has given us a free will and a mind that thinks and reasons and communicates freely with him.

One day during his ministry, Jesus was approached by a rich young man—successful, important, influential. He had already climbed to the top of the corporate ladder. He asked Jesus a question: "Teacher, what good thing must I do to get eternal life?" When Jesus told him to sell all his possessions and give to the poor, the young man "went away sad, because he had great wealth." What did Jesus do? He let the rich young man turn his back and walk away. Jesus didn't chase after him and demand that he sell his possessions and follow him. Jesus gave him the freedom to accept or reject his offer of eternal life (Matt. 19:16–26).

Similarly, in the garden of Eden, God allowed Adam and Eve to make their own choices. God gave them everything they needed, including the gift of free will. He had but one restriction: the tree that grew in the middle of the garden—"you must not touch it," he told them "or you will die" (Gen. 3:3). Unfortunately, both Adam and Eve made the terrible decision to eat the fruit of that tree, an action that sent them away from paradise and into a world of thorny weeds (v. 23).

"God seems to fly in the face of all caution," writes John Eldredge. "Even though he knew what would happen, when heartbreak and suffering and devastation would follow upon our disobedience, God chose to have children. And unlike some hyper-controlling parents, who take away every element of choice they can from their children, God gave us a remarkable choice. He did not make Adam and Eve obey him. He took a risk. A staggering risk, with staggering consequences."[6]

When King David saw beautiful Bathsheba bathing on her roof, God didn't strike David with blindness or impotence. God gave David free will to make his own choice. Unfortunately, David made a bad choice which led to more bad choices (2 Sam. 11).

When the prodigal son wanted his dad's retirement money to head for the far country, the loving father didn't chain him to the bedpost. He gave him the money, and he let him go. He took a risk. He simply blessed his son, and gave him wings and wallet (Luke 15:11–32).

God will never clip your wings. He wants you to fly, to remain in his love and follow his commands, but to grow up, mature spiritually, and produce fruit for his kingdom. "Now remain in my love . . . obey my commands . . . I chose you and appointed you to go and bear fruit—fruit that will last" (John 15:9–10, 16). "This is to my Father's glory," Jesus said, "that you bear much fruit, showing yourselves to be my disciples" (v. 8). Note that Jesus said *disciples*, not *robots*.

Our heavenly Father encourages his children to grow in their strengths and abilities in order to step into society and win a hurting world to Christ. He gives us these instructions, directives that use our talents and gifts to bring him glory: "Go and make disciples of all nations, baptizing them in the name of the Father and of the Son and of the Holy Spirit, and teaching them to obey everything I have commanded you" (Matt. 28:18–19).

Unlike your dad, "God does not want you to be His puppet. He wants you to be a strong, independent person who is able to choose life and make decisions."[7]

God wants you to make your own choices, always in the light of his Word, but needing no approval and affirmation from human others. You see, love itself is a risk, but it is a necessary component in a love relationship. Without risk, there is no genuine love. Love can't be coerced or forced. It cannot be clipped or caged. Love must encourage the loved one to develop wings and, when the time is right, to be parentally blessed and allowed to fly. A parent's blessing gives both roots and wings. And both are necessary to build a healthy, fruit-producing adult.

Chap and Dee Clark write: "To bless our children is to hand them a lifelong gift of emotional, relational, familial, and spiritual rootedness. When we express to our kids how we believe in them as people, we help create an environment where their minds and hearts are shaped according to that blessing."[8]

To that, I say amen.

Daily Sunlight

Your Personal Time to Grow:

Read Ecclesiastes 7:20. How does this verse help you to understand your imperfect father?

_____

_____

_____

What do you believe God the Father wants for you, his daughter?

_____

_____

_____

In what ways can you joyfully embrace the freedom God offers you? What do you think it will do for you?

_____

_____

_____

I believe *mint*, as a healing herb, best represents God's gift of freedom, as well as the strength he gives each of his daughters to pursue her individual calling and purpose. A popular seasoning herb in biblical days, Jewish leaders tithed mint (Luke 11:42). Mint thrives in all sorts of soil. It spreads rapidly, and is so hardy, not even winter snows kill it. Mint might represent the freedom, strength, and affirmation God gives each of his daughters. Our heavenly Father entrusts women to go courageously into all the world and produce fruit for him. I would suggest that you plant mint in your new garden.

Your Personal Prayer:

Father, thank you for giving me abundant freedom to make my own choices. You took a risk when you gave me free will. Rather than make me into a robot, you have allowed me to choose my path in life. I pray that I will choose to place my feet on your path, to place my total love and trust in you, my heavenly Father. Lead and guide me. You know the way I should go. Like the herb, mint, let me go boldly and grow fully and adapt well to all the situations you open up for me. Direct me to discover, pursue, and embrace your perfect will—to trust your ultimate goal for my life. In the name of your Son, amen.

Week 4: A Time to Trust, A Time to Embrace

Day 4: Amy, God promises you his presence

> The name *Jehovah Shammah* contains both promise and a sense of fulfillment. It focuses on God's personal presence as it relates to His purpose in the redemption of mankind.
>
> Ken Hemphill, *The Names of God*

On Day 5 of Week 2, I introduced you to Amy, a woman who suffered under an absentee workaholic dad who gave her plenty of "things," but didn't give her himself, his attention, his love or affection. Amy grew up feeling angry, unlovable, rejected, sad, lonely, and bitter. Amy's view of God? "I believe God is just like my dad," she said, "so busy running the universe that he has no time for anyone, especially me." (Please take a moment and briefly review her story.) Here is my letter to Amy.

Dear Amy:

Your heavenly Father's name is *Yahweh-Shammah*, meaning "the Lord is there" (Ezek. 48:35). God is, at the same time, above us, around us, and within us. We are never without his divine presence. He is closer than your hands and feet, and nearer than your breathing.

And, "in the New Testament we find names, such as *Immanuel* ('God with us') and *Abba* (Aramaic for 'Father'), that take our relationship with God to a whole new realm. Through Jesus Christ the Son and the Holy Spirit, God now dwells among and within his followers."[9]

God's Word makes promises to you about his constant presence—promises you can embrace and trust:

God is actively involved in your day-to-day life. He is never absent, but is an "ever-present help" (Ps. 46:1). He is always with you, helping you, strengthening you to do his work (Josh. 1:5). He is never disconnected or absent (Matt. 18:20), nor is he ever indifferent (John 3:16). He invites you to cast your cares on him (Ps. 55:22).

God will never drive you away from him (John 6:37), but will keep you until time itself ends (Matt. 28:20), and will call you his own (John 10:3, 11, 14).

He cares for you (1 Peter 5:7) so much that he keeps your tears in a bottle (Ps. 56:8). And one day he will wipe away all your tears (Rev. 7:17).

Surrounded by God's protecting presence, we need not be anxious or worry. He is an ever-present Friend who listens to us when we talk, who protects us when we walk, and who continually loves and comforts us.

My good friend, Carolyn Tomlin, tells about her father who so beautifully showed her the comforting qualities of God:

"Growing up in a Christian home, my father, Earl Ross, taught by example more than using words. His work was manual labor, consisting of painting barns and houses. After a hard day's work he still had time to listen to my childish chatter. Like other families of that era, we sat on the porch after dinner on summer evenings, talking until bedtime. I might ask about the stars and constellations, night sounds from insects or nocturnal animals, or why did moths hover around porch lights? And my father, in his wisdom, always had the answers.

"I recall a special memory of walking with my father down the road to the community general store. Between our home and the store lived a family with two large vicious dogs. I was terrified of their barking and snapping as we walked by. All I could see was those big teeth nipping at my ankles. My father always walked on the side next to the traffic until we reached this dwelling. Then as we approached the dogs, he took my hand in his and put himself between me and the dogs. Nothing was ever said. But I knew from past experience that my father was between me and danger. He was my comforter, my protector. And, how I loved him."

Surely, writes the apostle Paul in Philippians 4:10, "My God will meet all your needs according to his glorious riches in Christ Jesus." You can take his words to heart, and you can embrace them and trust them. You can allow him to fill that deep, empty, father-hungry hole.

Daily Sunlight

Your Personal Time to Grow:

Read Ecclesiastes 8:7–8. How does knowing that God is always present with you erase the fear Solomon's statements might cause? Explain.

_____

_____

_____

_____

Read Romans 8:38–39. What are those things that cannot separate you from God and his love? How do these promises comfort you? Encourage you? Give you security?

_____

_____

_____

_____

Philippians 4:10 tells you that God meets all your needs according to his glorious riches in Christ Jesus. Make a list of your current needs that you most want God to meet and why.

_____

_____

_____

_____

The next herb I suggest you plant in your new garden is *spikenard* (see Song 4:13–14; John 12:3), sometimes called nard. Traditionally believed to come from the Himalayas, this herb is known for its healing qualities and can represent God's heart-healing power as well as the rest and comfort his continual promised presence gives. Spikenard is the herb (made into a costly perfumed oil and described as an "alabaster jar of perfume" in Luke 7:37, 46) that the prostitute from Nain poured on Jesus' feet to anoint them (vv. 36–38). Mary of Bethany (John 12:1–8) also anointed Jesus' feet with spikenard shortly before his death. Judas objected to such extravagance when it could have been sold and the "money given to the poor." "It was worth a year's wages," he complained (v. 5). John writes: "The house was filled with the fragrance of the perfume" (v. 3). Surely, each woman's gift comforted Jesus and soothed his tired, dirty feet as its delicious fragrance lingered in the air.

Your Personal Prayer:

Father, your comforting presence reminds me of the healing herb spikenard. Your presence is priceless to me. Its comforting value cannot be described with mere words. Like spikenard, you heal my heart and calm my emotions and bring me peaceful rest. I need calm and rest, Father, as I strive to live in a violent, chaotic world. I need a whole heart and calm emotions as I reach out to minister to hurting others with your Word. Stay close to me. Gently lead me in the right direction. Teach me how to embrace your comfort and minister in your name. In Jesus' name, amen.

Week 4: A Time to Trust, A Time to Embrace

Day 5: Catherine, God's love cleanses you

> What kind of trust does a little girl place in her father? When she's two years old, he can put her on a ladder and say, "Come on, honey, jump and I'll catch you," and chances are that she'll do it without a second thought. She trusts him and knows that he would never allow her to be hurt. But when a father is molesting his daughter, he's letting that little girl hit the floor, and the injury that results can be devastating.
>
> Kevin Leman, *When Your Best Isn't Good Enough*

On Day 1 of Week 3, I introduced you to Catherine, a woman who suffered sexual abuse from a selfish father. His abuse produced within Catherine a deep sense of helplessness, hopelessness, and shame. She hates herself. She has few friends. She has no relationship with her heavenly Father. (Please take a moment and briefly review her story.) Here is my letter to Catherine.

Dear Catherine:

You told me you wanted no relationship with God, because he too carries the name "father." In your opinion, *father* is an "ugly word." You said you wanted nothing to do with God. And, you stated, "I am sure, he wants nothing to do with me."

You have been deeply wounded by your father. His heinous sins against you have influenced your marriage, career, and faith. His cruelty has greatly hurt you. But you need not continue to allow him to destroy your future. For you have a Father in heaven who loves you, who waits for you to come to him, and who will cleanse you from past shame and give you fresh hope.

Nancy Leigh DeMoss, in her insightful book *Lies Women Believe*, writes about your wonderful heavenly Father:

"If you have been wounded by a father—or another man you trusted—you may find it difficult to trust God. You may even be afraid of Him or angry with Him. You must believe me when I tell you that God is not like any man you have ever known. The wisest, kindest earthly father is but a pale reflection of our heavenly Father. The God of the Bible is infinitely more wonderful and pure and loving than even the most wonderful father. That is why it is so important that we not allow our view of God to be determined by other men, for at their very best they are flawed representations of God."[10]

Your father was flawed. He was not worthy of you or your trust. Now please don't allow your human father to ruin your relationship with your perfect and pure heavenly Father. That would be an even greater tragedy than a young life devastated by sexual abuse.

You feel burdened with shame. Did you know that "shame-burdened people are the sort whom Jesus had in mind when he invited the 'weary and heavy laden' to trade their heaviness for his lightness"?[11] (See Matt. 11:28–30.)

Throughout his life, Jesus offered cleansing and freedom to a number of women. He welcomed to himself those women who felt great shame, who had been used and abused and discarded. These women accepted his cleansing, treasured his love, and each began a new life embracing and trusting her heavenly Father. Consider these women mentioned in Scripture:

The Samaritan woman Jesus met at Jacob's Well. She had been hurt deeply, used and abused by five husbands, and then discarded like yesterday's crumpled newspaper. She had a thirst only her heavenly Father could fill. When Jesus offered her "living water,"she gulped it down, anxious to receive genuine love from her genuine Father. His living water cleansed her soul and washed away her shame (John 4:1–42).

The bleeding woman society shunned. As we saw earlier, this poor woman felt great shame, not for anything she had done, but from a sickness that caused her to bleed without relief. When Jesus came to town, she tiptoed up to him and touched his robe. He healed her, affirmed her faith, called her "daughter," and blessed her with peace (Mark 5:21–43).

Jesus' faithful follower Mary Magdalene. Mary was abused and tormented by seven indwelling demons (Luke 8:1–2). Jesus cast out those evil spirits and freed Mary from the pain and shame of Satan. Once she embraced Christ and became his faithful disciple, she followed him all the way to the cross when others retreated in fear (Mark 15:40–41). She went to his tomb two mornings later and Christ blessed her first with the good news of his resurrection (Mark 16:1–11; Luke 24:10; John 20:16).

Like these three women in Scripture, your shame has come to you by no fault of your own. You were a tender victim of sexual assault. You trusted your father, and he betrayed that trust for his own selfish sexual pleasure. His actions were not your fault nor are you responsible for them. He has a problem and must seek treatment for it. But now is the time to pull up those poisonous plants from your garden of shame. You need not let them grow there another hour. For God the Father waits to fill you with his "living water," to wash away your shame, to cleanse your soul, to restore your purity, to call you his "daughter," and to bless you with his remarkable peace.

Daily Sunlight

Your Personal Time to Grow:

Read Ecclesiastes 8:9. What does Solomon tell you about the person who purposely hurts others? Can you see how your father's oppression/cruelty/abuse of you has, in return, hurt him? If so, how?

_____

_____

_____

Recall an experience in which your father or another person purposely hurt you. Like Catherine, do you feel anger toward that person? If so, how does the anger impact you?

_____

_____

_____

What attributes of God the Father do you most need to embrace, and why?

_____

_____

_____

Plant *hyssop* (also called *marjoram*) in your new garden. It is the herb that heals and cleanses. Biblical worshipers used hyssop for ritual cleansing ceremonies (Lev. 14:4, 49). King David, in asking for forgiveness, prayed that God would "cleanse me with hyssop, and I will be clean; wash me, and I will be whiter than snow" (Ps. 51:7). Hyssop was also used as a digestive aid. And Israelites in Egypt used hyssop as a "brush of salvation" to spread blood on their doorposts to save them from the death angel (Ex. 12:22). You see, right now you allow the herb *nettle* to grow in your garden. Nettle (see Prov. 24:31; Isa. 34:13; Hos. 9:6) is a coarse, prickly plant with stinging, burning hairs. You must uproot the nettle, as well as many other hurtful plants, before you can replant.

Close your eyes for a moment and call to mind your imaginary garden. The weeds and nettles are gone, and the garden is empty. As you stand in the empty garden, envision yourself picking up a healing herb and placing it in the welcoming soil. Watch your hands as they tenderly pat good soil around the small plant. Pick up a watering can and shower the herb with water. Imagine the joy of watching it grow day by day—as you experience its beauty, grace, fragrance, and healing.

In your new garden, plant:

Saffron. Allow this healing herb to remind you of God's precious, valuable, unconditional love for you. Saffron is an expensive herb. God's love is also costly. It cost his Son, Jesus, his life.

Lavender. Brush your fingers against its lacy leaves. Notice how tall its long-stemmed violet flowers grow. Bend down and breathe in its gentle, sweet fragrance. Allow lavender to draw you to itself, and remind you that God is approachable, easy to talk to, and always just a prayer away.

Mint. It will grow fast, hardy, and will spread far and wide. It will thrive in rugged places and in harsh weather. Press your fingers into its small green leaves. Then bask in the fresh aroma it releases into the air around you. Allow mint to remind you that God gives you freedom to use your unique gifts to love and serve him. Each time you visit your garden, let mint affirm that God grants you both strength and ability to go out into the world and to produce fruit for him.

Spikenard. Expensive and fragrant, let this costly healing herb surround you with its lingering perfume. Rest in its refreshing aroma. Let it remind you of God's comforting presence—above you, beside you, and within you.

Hyssop. Allow it to cleanse you, wash away any shame or anger or pain that may still cause you sorrow. Let its healing qualities heal your soul and refresh your spirit.

Now, if you are ready, tell God of your desire to depend fully on his fatherly care:

"Father, I choose to trust and embrace your precious, valuable, unconditional love, kindness, compassion, and approachability for me because:

_____

_____

"Father, I choose to trust and embrace the strength, ability, freedom, and comforting presence you give me because:

_____

_____

"Father, I choose to trust and embrace your miraculous cleansing powers because:

_____

_____

Your Personal Prayer:

Father, I thank you for . . .

your unconditional love, in Christ Jesus, that nothing in all creation will be able to separate me from,

your generous saving grace,

your kindness, compassion, and approachability,

your everlasting love and drawing loving-kindness,

your freedom that allows me to remain in your love, obey your commands, and bear fruit that will last,

the privilege of being your disciple,

your wonderful presence and active involvement in my day-to-day life,

your names Yahweh-Shammah *and* Immanuel *that assure me of your nearness,*

your ever-present help,

your love that cleanses my shame, like it cleansed the Samaritan woman at Jacob's Well, the bleeding woman society shunned, and your faithful follower Mary Magdalene,

your precious Word that gives me help and hope in troubling times.

In Jesus' name I pray all these things, amen.

"A Time to Trust, A Time to Embrace"

Growing Together in God's Word:

1. Briefly share a highlight from the Week 4 "Daily Sunlight" sections, something that particularly spoke to you.

2. In Ecclesiastes 8:12–13, Solomon describes both "God-fearing" people and "wicked" people. Have you found his statements true in your own experience? If so, please explain.

_____

_____

_____

3. Describe how Jesus' encounters with ordinary people show his amazing approachability. What has Jesus shown you (or someone you know) about God's kindness and compassion?

_____

_____

_____

4. Do you know of someone who needs to embrace God's kindness, compassion, and approachability in her life today? If so (without using her name), describe that person, her past and/or present situation.

5. In John 15:1–6, Jesus describes himself as the Vine and his followers as branches that bear fruit. What does Jesus mean by this analogy? In what ways are you producing fruit?

_____

_____

6. Read the following Scriptures and describe what happened in each: Genesis 3:23; 2 Samuel 11; and Luke 15:11–32. If you were in God's place, would you have created people with freedom to choose? Why or why not?

_____

_____

_____

_____

7. Read the following: Ephesians 4:31; Hebrews 12:14–15; and James 3:14. What do these Scriptures tell us about bitterness?

_____

_____

_____

8. Do you know someone who feels bitterness? If so (without using her name), please explain why she feels bitterness. Discuss: what is the solution to her bitterness?

9. Have you ever felt anger, like Catherine, toward another person who purposely hurt you? If you would, describe that time. How did that person hurt you? Do you still feel anger toward him or her?

_____

_____

10. Describe how trusting God differs from trusting another person, especially one who has seriously wounded you in some way.

_____

_____

_____

Group Prayer:

Father, we pray for all hurting women everywhere. May they uproot the nettles that grow in their gardens. Those prickly plants have hurt them for a long time and harm them even now. May these women replant their gardens with healing hyssop, and know firsthand your thorough cleansing. May they drink your "living water" to wash away their shame—the pain caused by a sexually abusive father. Cleanse their souls, and restore their purity. Bless them with your remarkable peace. In the name of your Son, amen.

Week 5: A Time to Plant

Day 1: Gayle, God totally accepts you

> When . . . false and damaging expectations are recognized for what they
> are . . . then they can be rejected or modified. The result? No longer
> is another person setting the standard of perfection in life. Rather, an
> individual can seek to understand God's ways and perspectives on life—
> they are not weighty or burdensome.
>
> Charles Stanley, *Finding Peace*

On Day 2 of Week 3, I introduced you to Gayle, a woman who suffered under a harsh and critical father. In her father's eyes, Gayle could do nothing good enough to please him. He criticized her without relief. (Please take a moment and briefly review her story.) Here is my letter to Gayle.

Dear Gayle:

Your human father has done you a great injustice. He has warped your view of your heavenly Father. You stated that you see God as "a stern, hateful Father who sits in heaven and just watches for me to slip up and make a mistake." You admit, "I guess I'm as afraid of God the Father as I am my human father. I greatly respect them both, but I don't want to have anything to do with either of them."

Your human father punished you severely, criticized you constantly, and has turned you into a frustrated perfectionist—a people-pleaser. Your dad showed you nothing resembling grace or kindness. You are now void of self-esteem and self-confidence. When your dad so harshly criticized you, you felt as if you could never do anything right. You felt like you could never quite please him.

Let me assure you that God your heavenly Father is nothing like your human father. God loves you and accepts you. He does not criticize you, but gently guides you toward your potential. He disciplines all of his daughters because he longs for each to grow up and produce fruit for him. Let's look at how God relates to you in love.

God uses only loving and gentle discipline to teach us, his children, those things we most need to learn. Severe punishment and loving discipline are two different things. Punishment is a dead end. It makes a child bitter and sad. But loving discipline teaches a child to do right, and it does so without destroying a child's spirit. God's gentle discipline puts you back on the right track when you take a harmful detour. Scripture says: "Do not make light of the Lord's discipline, and do not lose heart when he rebukes you, because the Lord disciplines those he loves, and he chastens everyone he accepts as his child" (Heb. 12:5–6 TNIV).

Your father's methods of discipline degraded you as a daughter. Harsh and demeaning, not to mention embarrassing, they killed your spirit, and served no purpose. Perhaps your father learned this type of discipline from his own parents. Perhaps he knew no better. But whatever the reasons, his harsh and unloving discipline was wrong. It needlessly provoked you to anger, and caused you pain. It also pushed you away from your Father in heaven, a loss too great for any of God's precious daughters.

God your Father is the gentle shepherd (*Jehovah Rohi*—"the Lord is my Shepherd," Ps. 23:1) who protects you, who keeps you close to him in the fold, and who tenderly guides you back when you stray. Even though sometimes you may think God's discipline is painful, you and I must always trust him. He may strive to break your stubborn will, but he takes utmost care of your delicate spirit. "To be consistent with His nature, God must sometimes (in sorrow) chasten those He loves, but it is always with respect, dignity, and nobility—never in derision or ridicule."[1]

God is an encourager, not a critic. Criticism from someone you love, even constructive criticism, is often hard to hear. When we do our best, you and I want to hear praise, not be told we're not perfect. How often can we take to heart another's negative remarks, especially if delivered in a less than loving way? We tend to believe we are "worthless" and "not important." We can feel as if our spirit has been trampled into the dirt.

God wants to nurture your spirit, not destroy it. God wants you to do your best in all you do, but he never expects or demands perfection. You have become harder on yourself than your father ever was. You have become the critic that never stops shouting in your ear: "Do it better! It's not good enough! You're not good enough! You are a failure!" You must silence that inner critic, the voice that beats you down. It is not from God.

God shows you grace, not the condemnation your human father showed you. He totally accepts you—just as you are. What is grace? It is the gift of a loving Parent. My favorite definition of grace comes from Philip Yancey: "Grace means there is nothing I can do to make God love me more, and nothing I can do to make God love me less. It means that I, even I who deserve the opposite, am invited to take my place at the table in God's family."[2]

As a child, you looked up to your human father and desperately needed his grace and encouragement. Instead you received his criticism and discouragement. How fortunate is the child who has a father she can truly trust.

But it's not too late for you to experience God's grace. Lewis Smedes writes: "To experience grace is to recover our lost inner child. The heart of our inner child is trust. We lose our childhood when we feel that the persons we trusted to accept us do not accept us or that they may reject us if we do things that displease them. Shame cheats us of childhood. Grace gives it back to us."[3]

When a girl receives no grace from her human father, when she is routinely criticized and not encouraged, she tends to become a perfectionist. As a perfectionistic girl grows up, she pushes herself "to do everything better, to accomplish more and more, to work after some sense of perfect satisfaction that no human can experience. The perfectionist's favorite expressions are 'I should . . . ,' 'I have to . . . ,' and 'I must. . . .' [Perfectionists] never have any peace of mind because they can never achieve perfection. Their overwhelming need to accomplish more and more makes them driven, stressed, and irritable."[4] The perfectionist daughter also sees God as a strict, driving slavemaster who expects perfection and will settle for nothing else. Even prayer and personal devotions become times of accomplishing magnanimous to-do lists.

Another danger exists when fathers fail to parent with grace, when they fail to affirm growing daughters: these women "are more likely to be promiscuous and less likely to commit to long-term relationships."[5]

You can become withdrawn, wounded, critical of others, and feel no sense of acceptance from others or from yourself. When you are unduly pressured by a harsh father, you can fail to become the woman God intends. Your father's criticism may even destroy you, and you may never realize a sense of fulfillment in your life. Relaxation, play, and fun will elude you if you constantly push yourself to achieve more and more. You will find instead un-fulfillment, frustration, and exhaustion. Even your successes will not satisfy you. Unless you decide to make a tough change, you will live your life in deep discouragement.

Jesus holds out his hand to you and promises, "My yoke is easy and my burden is light" (Matt. 11:30). Embrace him. Trust him. Plant in your new garden his gentleness and grace.

Daily Sunlight

Your Personal Time to Grow:

In Ecclesiastes 8:14, Solomon makes a statement about the "righteous" and the "wicked." Have you seen this happen? Describe the situation. How did it influence you?

_____

_____

_____

_____

The Psalms are filled with reminders of God's love and mercy. Choose three of the following verses to read and ponder: 4:1; 5:7; 6:4; 9:13; 21:7; 25:6; 26:11; 30:10. What do these verses say to you?

_____

_____

_____

_____

If you are a "perfectionist daughter," how do you view God as Father, and why?

_____

_____

_____

_____

What does author Lewis Smedes and his description of "lost grace" say to you?

_____

_____

_____

_____

What healing herb does this garden need? *Aloe vera.* As early as 1500 BC, Egyptians used aloe vera as a medicine. Even today it is used to treat sores and burns, and soothe damaged skin. It's an amazing herb. Did you know that "the aloe leaf contains over 75 nutrients and 200 active compounds, including 20 minerals, 18 amino acids, and 12 vitamins"?[6] Aloe vera well represents God's healing mercy, his gentle discipline, and his everlasting comfort. It is especially comforting if your father left your soul with the open sores caused by sharp criticism and harsh discipline.

Your Personal Prayer:

Father, I have learned that caustic criticism from a loved one can hurt my very soul. My wounds are deep. May I forever know that you are kind and gentle in your discipline, that you are an encourager—not a critic, that you offer a "yoke" that is easy and light. Thank you for your healing grace—a gift I could never deserve, but one that you give freely and lovingly. I pray this prayer in the name of Jehovah Rohi, *amen.*

Week 5: A Time to Plant

Day 2: Faye, God is dependable—he keeps his word

> "Do not worry about tomorrow."
> Jesus in Matthew 6:34

On Day 3 of Week 3, I introduced you to Faye, a woman who suffered under an undependable dad. (Please take a moment and briefly review her story.) Here is my letter to Faye.

Dear Faye:

Growing up with a weak dad, you said you also viewed God as "a weak, inept Father that I don't dare depend on." But know this: God your Father is dependable. He keeps his word. He has the strength and power to make and keep promises. His name is *Elohim* (Gen. 1:1), which means "that God alone is eternal" and "powerful."[7] His name is also *Yahweh-Yireh*: "The Lord will provide." (This name was used in Genesis 22:14 when Abraham prepared to sacrifice his son Isaac and God provided a ram to take Isaac's place as the offering.)

You need not worry about those things you need to sustain your life and the lives of your children. God provides you, his daughter, with everything you need. He invites you to trust him.

Jesus spoke to a crowd of people on a mountainside one day. Maybe he sensed they were worriers, and that they needed to know that God is dependable and able to provide for them. He told them, "Do not worry about your life, what you will eat or drink; or about your body, what you will wear" (Matt. 6:25). He asked them this question: "Is not life more important than food, and the body more important than clothes?"

I like to think that as Jesus spoke, a cluster of birds flew by. Perhaps he pointed to the sky, smiled at the carefree winged creatures, and told his listeners: "Look at the birds of the air; they do not sow or reap or store away in barns, and yet your heavenly Father feeds them." He asked them another question: "Are you not much more valuable than they?" (v. 26)

Perhaps Jesus glanced to his left and saw a field of beautiful lilies growing in the sunlight. "And why do you worry about clothes?" he asked. "See how the lilies of the field grow. They do not labor or spin. Yet I tell you that not even Solomon in all his splendor was dressed like one of these" (vv. 28–29). Then Jesus made them a promise to prove God's dependability: "If that is how God clothes the grass of the field, which is here today and tomorrow is thrown into the fire, will he not much more clothe you, O you of little faith?" (v. 30).

Jesus closed with this advice: "So, do not worry, saying 'What shall we eat?' or 'What shall we drink?' or 'What shall we wear?' For the pagans run after all these things, and your heavenly Father knows that you need them. But seek first his kingdom and his righteousness, and all these things will be given to you as well" (vv. 31–33). As if to be sure the people understood, he added: "Therefore do not worry about tomorrow, for tomorrow will worry about itself. Each day has enough trouble of its own" (v. 34).

After hearing Jesus' message on the dependability of God as Provider, I would imagine that every time one of his listeners saw a bird fly by or saw a lily growing in a field, each one remembered Jesus' words of assurance. And each would be reminded anew that God is dependable. He keeps his word to his children. And he can be trusted.

One of my favorite people in church history is Martin Luther, the great Protestant Reformer, who sought, some 500 years ago, to transform the Roman Catholic Church. Listen as he comments on this passage of Scripture: "You see, He is making the birds our schoolmasters and teachers.... Now Christ says: 'Every day you see before your very eyes how the heavenly Father feeds the little birds in the field, without any concern on their part. Can you not trust Him to feed you as well, since He is your Father and calls you His children? Shall He not be concerned about you, whom He has made His children and to whom He gives His Word and all creatures, more than about the little birds, which are not His children but your servants? And yet He thinks enough of them to feed them every day, as if they were the only thing He is concerned about.... Now, since the birds have learned so well the art of trusting Him and of casting their cares from themselves upon God, we who are His children should do so even more.'"[8]

Martin Luther also had something significant to say about the lilies Jesus talked about. "Just look at them grow," Luther writes, "all adorned with lovely colors! Yet not one of them is anxious or worried about how it should grow or what color it should have, but it leaves these anxieties to God. And without any care or effort on its part God dresses it up in such lovely and beautiful colors that, as Christ says, King Solomon in all his glory was not so beautiful as one of these. . . . Now, since He dresses and adorns so many flowers with such a variety of colors, and each has its own coat, more splendid than all the adornment in the world, why is it that we cannot have faith that He will dress us as well?"[9]

The time has come for you to replant God's healing herbs in your life garden. Depend on this: "the Holy Spirit moves us to look to God as our Father and trust Him as a secure child trusts a dependable parent." What does this mean for your life? "This means leaving former childhood patterns that are interfering with the way in which you are currently experiencing life."[10]

It means that you can relax. You can stop pushing yourself to accomplish everything and to do it all perfectly. You can learn to depend on your heavenly Father who promises to provide for your needs. Trust God to help you do this.

Daily Sunlight

Your Personal Time to Grow:

Read Ecclesiastes 9:1–6, which describes how death comes to all people. If your father has already died, what are your favorite memories of him? What unpleasant memories do you remember about him? If your father is living, ponder what he will leave you to remember. Is it good or bad?

_____

_____

_____

_____

_____

Read Psalm 40. What did the Lord do specifically for David, and what do you want the Lord to do specifically for you right now?

_____

_____

_____

_____

_____

_____

Read Psalm 54:4. For what reason did David cry out for the Lord to save him? Name a time when you have called out to the Lord for help. What was the situation? What help did he give you?

_____

_____

_____

_____

Read Psalm 100:5. What does the psalmist proclaim about God's goodness, love, and faithfulness? Name a time when God was especially good, loving, and faithful to you.

_____

_____

_____

_____

_____

Plant *black cumin* in your garden. It's an herb so dependable and healing that an old Arab proverb calls it "the medicine for every disease except death"! In biblical days, women mixed black cumin in bread and cakes. They depended on it to purge the body of worms and parasites, and relieve the symptoms of asthma, bronchitis, and coughs. It has been used for thousands of years to heal everything from abscesses of the stomach to tumors of the eyes and liver. This ancient herb could well represent God's dependability, power, and promised strength.

Your Personal Prayer:

Father, in this day of scary uncertainty, I need to know I can put my trust in your Word. I need to know that you are dependable, Father. You are Elohim and Yahweh-Yireh, and I can depend on your limitless power and your dependable provision. Thank you that I can lean on your love and totally trust you. In Jesus' name, amen.

Day 3: Priscilla, God will never abandon you

> In our Father, God, we have absolute stability and security. We have a parent who is consistently wise and good, and our position as His children is assured.
>
> H. Norman Wright, *Making Peace with Your Past*

On Day 4 of Week 3, I introduced you to Priscilla, a woman who suffered with a deadbeat dad who eventually abandoned his family. (Please take a moment and briefly review her story.) Here is my letter to Priscilla.

Dear Priscilla:

An absent dad often can mean an unsettling and insecure future. Little girls especially can feel like orphans—unloved, uncared for, unguarded, alone, and defenseless. When dads disappear from families, they often take away a child's provision and protection. While single mothers, grandmothers, or other family members can do a great job caring for children, a loving mom *and* dad can give a child more security, and a greater sense of family and refuge when troubles come.

As a child, you were in no way responsible for your dad's abandonment. While his leaving without explanation has caused you a problem, *you* are *not* the problem. *He* has the problem, and while you can pray for him and forgive him, *you* cannot make *his* problem go away. He responded to his children and wife in an irresponsible way. In the long run, he is the loser, and his loss of family may haunt him for a lifetime.

Even though your human father abandoned you, God your heavenly Father will never abandon you. He calls you to believe him, to trust him and his Word. The Lord is your security. He is your shelter. You can declare assuredly with the psalmist: "He is my refuge and my fortress, my God, in whom I trust. . . . He will cover you with his feathers, and under his wings you will find refuge; his faithfulness will be your shield and rampart" (Ps. 91:2, 4).

How interesting that the psalmist uses these specific descriptions of our Father's protection: a refuge, fortress, shield, and rampart. Each is an image describing one's protection in war, or when invaded by an enemy:

Refuge:	A shelter from an enemy's threat of death or destruction.
Fortress:	Both ancient and current civilizations have depended on forts to shield them from an enemy. In biblical days, people fortified their entire cities with tall, strong walls, usually built with rocks and limestone blocks. Whenever danger threatened, everybody who lived outside the city's fortified walls would run inside the fortress (see Jer. 4:5; 8:14).
Shield:	A piece of armor carried on the arm or in the hand to defend a soldier against an enemy's sword, mace (a war club used to crush the head), arrow, javelin, or spear. In ancient days, soldiers made shields from wicker or leather stretched over wooden frames with handles inside. They often attached metal plates to the front for extra strength.
Rampart:	A barrier or embankment (usually made of earth) that encircled a fortress to guard it from an attacking enemy. Sometimes called a bulwark.

But isn't it interesting that within the same sentence, the psalmist shows not only God's *powerful strength* (with the use of military objects), but also shows his *nurturing protection* with the image of a mother hen—her wings extended around her young brood of defenseless chicks? Jesus also used this motherly image when he tearfully lamented over Jerusalem's refusal to believe in him as God's Son: "O Jerusalem, Jerusalem," he cried, "you who kill the prophets and stone those sent to you, how often I have longed to gather your children together, as a hen gathers her chicks under her wings, but you were not willing" (Matt. 23:37).

Authors Thad and Erilynne Barnum write: "Psalm 91 is a psalm of faith. It calls the believer to trust the Lord. It assures the faithful, for all time, that the Lord is our security in a time of trouble. No matter what the circumstance, no matter how difficult the situation, He is our shelter."[11]

But instead of guarding you, your earthly father abandoned you. In a very real sense, he rejected you. "The only way we can overcome the fear of rejection is to focus on the reality of God's acceptance of us based on our position in Christ rather than on the approval of others based on our performance," writes Robert McGee.[12]

Let's focus for a moment on this scriptural reality. In his Word, God promises:

Scripture	God's Promise
James 4:8	If we come near to him, he will respond in the same way: he will come near to us.
Psalm 46:1, 7	"God is our refuge and strength, an ever-present help in trouble. . . . The LORD Almighty is with us; the God of Jacob is our fortress."
Psalm 61:4	David, whose enemies constantly threatened his life and safety, tells the Lord: "I long to dwell in your tent forever, and take refuge in the shelter of your wings."
Mark 10:16	Jesus showed special consideration to the young, defenseless children of his day. He often "took the children in his arms, put his hands on them and blessed them."

Not only does God accept you and protect you, he assures you that, as a believer in Christ, you are his child. You might feel that you had no value to your dad, that you were not worth his love, time, and attention. You may think that if your own father rejected you, other people may also deem you worthless and reject you as well. You may even reject yourself. Know that God, your heavenly Father, will never reject you. You, his dear daughter, as a believer in Christ, are more than accepted—you are *chosen* by him to be part of his family.

I wish you had had a dad who stayed on the job of rearing you, and showed you, by example, your true Father in heaven. It is so true that "a father has great power over his daughter. For most daughters, he holds the key to such life issues as self-esteem, career choices and ambition, relational stability, behavior and expectations in dating and marriage, and the ability to see herself as a fully functioning adult."[13]

You have discovered this truth in your own life, and you have been deeply scarred. But you need not hold on to those scars, for "a loving, involved, attentive father can save his daughter from a lifetime of painful and destructive experiences. A girl who grows up with the perception that her father loves her, believes in her, trusts her, and celebrates the unique person that she is has a much better chance at reaching her God-given potential than one who is left to fend for herself."[14]

You have such a Father, and he loves you, believes in you, and celebrates the unique person that you are. He is your heavenly Father.

Don't allow a deadbeat dad to color your perception of yourself, men in general, or your heavenly Father. Come near to God. Know with full assurance that his love and care are forever. Be secure in the shelter of his acceptance. Feel proper esteem that he chose you as one of his own. Find shelter and security within his enveloping wings, for you are one of his beloved brood.

Daily Sunlight

Your Personal Time to Grow:

What advice does the writer of Ecclesiastes give in 9:7–10? What else might you add to his list?

_____

_____

_____

God's Word tells us that we are genuine heirs, eternally adopted into his family. The apostle Paul writes: "The Spirit himself testifies with our spirit that we are God's children . . .heirs of God and co-heirs with Christ" (Rom. 8:16–17). Describe what it feels like to know your legitimacy as a daughter in his eternal family.

_____

_____

_____

As a good and involved Father, God will guide you, strengthen you, and satisfy your needs (see Isa. 58:11–12). He will make you "like a well-watered garden, like a spring whose waters never fail." In biblical times, water was scarce. With that knowledge, why do you think Scripture uses the example of "well-watered gardens" and unlimited "spring waters" to describe God's goodness and involvement in your life?

_____

_____

_____

In what ways does God "guide you," "strengthen you," and "satisfy your needs"? Give several examples, both recent and past.

_____

_____

_____

_____

_____

I believe *frankincense*—a historic herbal oil with numerous healing properties—is the herb to plant in your garden. Frankincense has a rich history. Used as holy anointing oil to enhance meditation, it was also used to make holy incense for Moses' tabernacle (Ex. 30:31, 34). Worshipers found great security, and a certain pattern of stability, when they stepped into their places of worship and breathed in the familiar perfumed incense. Perhaps frankincense can also represent a promise. Zacharias was in the temple burning frankincense when the angel Gabriel visited him and told him of his son John's upcoming birth (Luke 1:9–10). When the Magi visited the Christ child, they brought him frankincense—a promise of salvation God made long ago to a waiting world (Matt. 2:10–11). God makes promises to you today too—the promise of his eternal Fatherhood, his daily strength, and his satisfying provision.

Another healing herb for your garden might be *chamomile*. When made into a tea, this herb will soothe your mind and body and help you to sleep. Imagine the security of a sound sleep when you know God is always present, watching over you, and will never leave you.

Your Personal Prayer:

Father, thank you for adopting me into your eternal family through your Son, Jesus; for calling me your precious daughter whom you love and care for; for guiding and strengthening me and satisfying my needs; for promising me you'll never leave me alone and abandoned; for giving me the security and stability of your love and presence; and for allowing me to sleep clothed securely in your perfect peace. In the name of your Son, amen.

Week 5: A Time to Plant

Day 4: Karen, God is trustworthy—he never changes

> Fathers are family leaders, and truthfulness and trustworthiness produce
> the kind of consistency that creates peace and stability in a family.
>
> Kenneth O. Gangel and Jeffrey S. Gangel, *Fathering Like the Father*

On Day 5 of Week 3, I introduced you to Karen, a woman who endured a childhood with an untrustworthy, drug- and alcohol-addicted dad. (Please take a moment and briefly review her story.) Here is my letter to Karen.

Dear Karen:

You've been hurt in many ways by your dad's drug and alcohol addictions. You discovered early in your childhood that you couldn't trust him. You never knew when he would become violent, loud, and abusive. Trust is significantly important between a father and daughter. It means that she can depend on his integrity and character. She can put her confidence and sense of security, her faith and hope in him. You weren't able to do that.

Through your dad's untrustworthiness, he distorted your view of God. You now believe that your heavenly Father is as unreliable as your dad. That is unfortunate.

You also are the victim of a divorce. Much has been written on the effects of divorce on children. Consider for a moment the results from a long-term study by Dr. Judith Wallerstein: "The effects of divorce on children are not short-term and transient. They are long-lasting, profound, and cumulative. . . . [Children of divorce] view their parents differently, and they have lingering fears about their ability to commit to relationships that affect their own marriages." Dr. Wallerstein has found that whereas divorcing spouses may go through intense pain for three or less years after divorce, the effects of the divorce for children may last for decades. Children of divorce are "more likely to struggle with drugs, alcohol, and sex, . . . some as early as age 14."[15]

Because of your dad's addictions and the divorce, you had no quality male leadership in your family. Your family knew no consistency, stability, or peace. But this need not be permanent. Why? Because your Father in heaven—who never changes—can change you!

One of God's attributes is that he is *immutable. Immutable* means unchanging. God is unchanging in nature, desire, and purpose. God stays the same even while everything else in creation is changing. God your heavenly Father will never let you down. He'll never divorce you or leave you. Unlike your human father's "Dr. Jekyll, Mr. Hyde" moodiness, God's temperament stays the same throughout eternity. Scripture also promises us that God's words are trustworthy, that although heaven and earth will one day pass away, God's words will not fail or pass away (Matt. 5:18; 24:35.)[16]

Here are some of Scripture's promises:

Promise	Scripture Verse
As his believing daughter, you will be with him forever:	"If we have been united with him like this in his death, we will certainly also be united with him in his resurrection . . . now if we died with Christ, we believe that we will also live with him" (Rom. 6:5, 8).
God works actively, and for good purposes, in your everyday life:	"And we know that in all things God works for the good of those who love him, who have been called according to his purpose" (Rom. 8:28).
God is on your side, and he cares for you:	"If God is for us, who can be against us? He who did not spare his own Son, but gave him up for us all—how will he not also, along with him, graciously give us all things?" (Rom. 8:31–32).
God is worth your total trust:	"Trust in God; trust also in me" (John 14:1). "Trust in the LORD with all your heart and lean not on your own understanding" (Prov. 3:5). "These words are trustworthy and true" (Rev. 22:6).

God's trustworthiness provides a "quiet knowing" within you—a sense of inner peace and serenity. Gigi Tchividjian and Ruth Graham write: "A quiet knowing is . . . a sense of serenity. Most people [we] know are desperately searching for a sense of serenity. Serenity is that inner peace that comes with the certainties of knowing in whom you believe, what you believe, who you are, and where you're going."[17]

God will not let you down. He will not disappoint you. Only he can fulfill your heart's deepest longings for a trustworthy Father and create within you that sense of prevailing quietness and peace. In his book *Finding Peace*, Charles Stanley writes: "God's peace comes to them when they are united by faith with God . . . a prevailing sense of quietness and rest in a person's heart and emotions—of being unperturbed and unruffled. Peace is synonymous with being tranquil, serene, untroubled, and calm. It is a very real 'state' of the soul."[18]

You can know that God the Father believes in you and loves you. You can trust him totally. As a perfect Father, the Lord can give you confidence and set you on the right path. He can give you a purpose—to do his work on earth. He alone can fill that empty void in your heart. God the Father has made you for himself. Trust him.

Daily Sunlight

Your Personal Time to Grow:

What is meant by a "quiet knowing"? Have you experienced this "sense of serenity" described by Gigi Tchividjian and Ruth Graham? If so, describe it. If you haven't experienced it, imagine what it would be like.

_____

_____

_____

_____

_____

What is your personal meaning of peace? Do you know and experience God's peace in your life? If so, describe it.

_____

_____

_____

_____

In your new garden, plant *cinnamon*. Did you know that God provided the children of Israel with *cinnamomum* (from two species of *cinnamon* and *cassia*) while they wandered for forty years through the wilderness? Cinnamon/cassia contain agents that support the human immune system against influenza and colds. God's trustworthiness kept his children healthy and well as he led them toward the Promised Land. They could experience God's peace, quietness, and serenity even in the midst of danger and disease.

Your Personal Prayer:

Father, thank you for being trustworthy. You deal with me in a truthful way, a way I can truly depend on. Please continue to bless me with your stability and peace. Even in this uncertain world, I know that I can trust you, and that I can put my complete trust in your Word. In Jesus' name, amen.

Week 5: A Time to Plant

Day 5: Trusting God, your ultimate Father-Gardener

> We never outgrow our need for an accepting parent. . . . Realizing that
> God is our heavenly Father—the kind of father a father should be—can
> give us deep emotional satisfaction.
>
> H. Norman Wright, *Making Peace with Your Past*

What have you discovered (through my letters to Alexandra, Joyce, Bethany, Amy, Catherine, Gayle, Faye, Priscilla, and Karen) about God, your ultimate Father? Have you figured out that you can trust God completely? Today, I want to review God's promises to you, his daughter. Let's look again, in more detail, at the Father's firm and reliable characteristics—his personal attributes that you can wholeheartedly trust:

God has made himself known to you, his unique creation, through Jesus Christ. He desires an intimate Father-daughter relationship with you. By believing and trusting in Jesus as your personal Lord and Savior, God adopts you into his eternal family (John 3:16). Even if you've known only insecurity from your earthly father, you can know complete security in God's family, for God is trustworthy and dependable, and nothing can separate you— his daughter—from his love and care. While "insecurity is depending upon temporal things that we have no right or ability to control, security is depending on eternal life and values that no one or no thing can take away from us."[19] You can put your trust in God's security even when nothing else in this world is secure.

God loves you with an unconditional love. Unlike your human father's conditional love, based on performance, God loves and accepts you just as you are. "Conditional love allows for no mistakes," writes Reeni Fenholt. "Conditional love is for perfect people who do everything right. Mistakes must stay hidden; therefore, not even repentance is acceptable. You're loved or not loved for what you do; not for who you are or who you can become. . . . It is a taskmaster."[20] What is unconditional love? It is an accepting love. "Unconditional love is the commitment that says, 'I will stay with you no matter what. I will always love you. I will affirm you and support you.' Acceptance means, 'I will receive you even in the midst of tough times.' . . . We need unconditional love," write Gary and Barbara Rosberg. "Love that won't quit. We need to know we are accepted even when we come up short, even when we can't see beyond our own pain and failures."[21] You can open your heart to your heavenly Father, and trust that he will love you and accept you—wounds, faults, warts and all.

God is not limited in any way. He is self-existent and needs nothing. He is completely self-sufficient within himself (Ps. 36:9; John 5:26). God is not ruled by anyone or anything. He is not controlled or limited by time (he is eternal), or space (he has access to the whole of creation at all times (Ps. 139:7–12; Acts 17:24–25). He possesses all knowledge—past, present, and future (Ps. 147:5; Rom. 11:33). God has no need to learn, because he knows all. God has all power over his creation. He does not grow tired or weary (Isa. 40:28; Jer. 32:17). He is the Supreme Being in the universe, and he works everything out according to his will and purpose (Eph. 1:11).

God does not change. You can trust and rely upon his consistent nature. "To affirm that God is consistent means He never becomes greater, better, or worse; He never learns, grows, develops, improves, evolves, or gets younger or older. While He is consistent, He is not static or isolated from His creation but dynamic and involved with His creation."[22]

God is holy. You can trust him to be completely unique, pure, and faithful. He keeps his promises (Ps. 105:42). He is righteous, just, and truthful. You can trust his word. His actions are true and steadfast. God deals in grace and mercy—gifts we, as sinful humans, do not deserve (Eph. 1:7–8; 2:8; Titus 3:4–7). His love for us is persistent, patient, and kind (Rom. 2:4; 2 Peter 3:9). He initiates love (1 John 4:7–10) long before we express our love to him.

God is kind and compassionate, patient and slow to anger. You can trust him even though "it's tough to understand that God is loving, compassionate, protective, and gracious when our parents weren't that way."[23] God, your heavenly Father, is always actively working in your life. He cares for you as the unique individual he created you to be. He has a purpose for you in this life—to bear eternal fruit for him. He doesn't expect perfection from you. He only asks that you "work hard and cheerfully at whatever you do, as though you were working for the Lord rather than for people" (Col. 3:23 NLT). And when you fail, he forgives you, picks you up off the ground, dusts you off, and gives you another chance to do your best for him. Norman Wright writes: God "loves me with a love that is not turned off by my sins, my failures, my inadequacies, my insignificance. . . . I am a [person] beloved by God Himself. I have touched the very heart of the universe, and have found His name to be love. And that love has reached me, not because I have merited God's favor, not because I have anything to boast about, but because of what He is, and because of what Christ has done for me in the Father's name."[24]

As women, we need a human father who demonstrates to us the attributes and nature of God our Father. Normajean Hinders writes: "Of all the sources for approval and gaining a sense of well-being a father's voice is one of the loudest. Young women who perceive their fathers to be supportive and encouraging embrace their emerging womanhood and weather the rough ego–teen years with relatively few bumps and bruises. Whereas, daughters of fathers with critical voices have little defense to run behind when . . . their worth is callously attacked. A father's voice calls his daughter to be the best she can be. His voice of love allows her soul to rest. His balanced authority provides safety. Otherwise, she struggles to find from other men and in other places the approval she yearns for from her father."[25]

This kind of human father, of course, is the ideal. But many women haven't had a loving father. Perhaps you yourself had no father who showed you the love, protection, approval, support, and encouragement of God's nature. If not, you can know and trust that you have a perfect and loving heavenly Father who adopts you—through his Son, Jesus—into his eternal family.

You and I can "trust in the LORD forever, for the LORD, the LORD, is the Rock eternal" (Isa. 26:4).

Daily Sunlight

Your Personal Time to Grow:

Read Ecclesiastes 11:7–10, which talks about living life to the fullest despite hard times. How easy is it for you to do this? What do you think is the secret to success in this area? (See Eccl. 12:1, 13.)

_____

_____

_____

_____

_____

_____

In Week 4 you "planted" saffron, lavender, mint, spikenard, and hyssop in your imaginary new garden. Now I invite you to ask God to help you "plant" those attributes of his you studied this week:

"Father, I choose to plant *aloe vera* in my new garden to represent your healing mercy, gentle discipline, and everlasting comfort. Aloe vera can soothe my sore, painful skin made raw by sharp criticism and harsh discipline. I need your mercy, discipline, and comfort right now because I believe it will heal me in the following ways:

_____

_____

"Father, I choose to plant *black cumin* in my new garden. This ancient, dependable herb beautifully represents your *Elohim* and *Yahweh-Yireh* dependability, power, and strength. I need your dependability, power, and strength right now because I believe it will heal me in the following ways:

_____

_____

"Father, I choose to plant *frankincense* in my new garden. I believe it is the healing, herbal oil that best represents your security, stability, and satisfying provision in an uncertain world. I need your security, stability and provision right now because I believe it will heal me in the following ways:

_____

_____

"Father, I choose to plant *chamomile* in my new garden because it best represents your gift of healing, presence, and nearness. I need your healing, presence, and nearness right now because I believe it will help me in the following ways:

_____

_____

"Father, I choose to plant *cinnamon/cassia* in my new garden as I believe it represents your bountiful trustworthiness and continued care for me. I need your trustworthiness and care right now because I believe it will heal me in the following ways:

_____

_____

In your imagination, stand back and look at your new, fully planted garden. As you bend down and touch each tender herb, ask God to care for this particular plant, to allow it to grow strong and abundant in your garden, to use it to bring healing to you and to give you freedom from your past pain.

Do you see the beauty of your new garden? You have uprooted and thrown away past hurtful plants, and you have chosen and planted healing herbs you now need in your life. View the fresh landscape. Now is the time to nurture your seedling herbs, to keep them staked straight and strong, to keep them watered and fertilized, and to help them grow deep roots and strong stems. Nurture these young seedlings, and one day they will produce the fruits that bring peace to your life, and healing to the lives of all you reach out and touch with Christ's love.

Your Personal Prayer:

Father, I thank you for your healing mercy, gentle discipline, and everlasting comfort; for your dependability, power, and strength; for your security, stability, and continual thoughtful provision; for your gift of healing, your presence, and your eternal nearness; for your trustworthiness, closeness, and loving care. Father, you are the great teacher, and the one who corrects me kindly when I need to be chastened. You are the gentle shepherd — Jehovah Rohi — who keeps me close to the fold and guides me back home when I stray. You are the great encourager who loves me, forgives me, and accepts me even when I stumble, fall, and fail. You are the dependable one, the generous giver of grace and mercy. I trust your eternal words of assurance, and I do not worry about today or tomorrow. You are the great provider who cares for me like the birds of the air and the lilies of the field. You are the Father who will never abandon or leave me. You are my refuge, fortress, shield, and rampart. You are the one who covers me with your wings and protects me from my enemies. You are, at the same time, powerful and nurturing. You are unchanging and constant. You produce in me a soul-rest serenity and peace. You are holy, Father. I love and trust you, and find that life in you is indeed sweet. In the name of your Son, amen.

"A Time to Plant"

Growing Together in God's Word:

1. Briefly share a highlight from the Week 5 "Daily Sunlight" sections, something that particularly spoke to you.

2. You have read most of the book of Ecclesiastes during the past four weeks. Why do you think the author wrote this book? What is its meaning to you?

_____

_____

3. Two of God's names are *Elohim* and *Yahweh-Yireh*. In what ways do *Elohim* and *Yahweh-Yireh* describe God and his character? In what ways do these names give you security and cause you to rest?

_____

_____

4. Take turns reading aloud the following Scriptures: James 4:8; Psalm 46:1, 7; 61:4; Isaiah 58:11–12; Mark 10:16; Romans 8:16–17; Ephesians 1:4–5; James 4:8; and 1 John 3:1. Then note God's promises included within these verses. Name the promises you most treasure in your life, and tell why.

_____

_____

5. First John 3:1 tells us that the Father's love has been lavished on us, and that he himself calls us his children. What is a father's responsibility toward his children? What is a daughter's responsibility toward her father? In what ways has God the Father "lavished" his love on you?

_____

_____

6. Paul assures us in Ephesians 1:4–5 that God chose us to be his beloved children before he created the world. He has adopted us through Jesus Christ because he loves us. In your opinion, what does "adoption" mean? What are the responsibilities of adoptive parents to their chosen children?

_____

_____

7. This past week, we learned that: (1) God is the Supreme Being of the universe and is all-powerful over it; (2) he has no need to learn, because he knows everything; (3) he does not grow tired or weary; and (4) he works out everything according to his will and purpose. What should these truths mean to us in our everyday lives?

_____

_____

Group Prayer:

Father, point out to us those harmful, poisonous plants that are causing pain in our lives. Teach us how to pull them up by the roots so they won't grow back "mean and strong." Choose for us those therapeutic herbs that you want us to replant in our lives so that we can allow your love, trust, dependability, and nurture to bring us soul-healing, new growth, and peace. In Jesus' name, amen.

Week 6: A Time to Heal, A Time for Peace

Day 1: A time to search—seeking to understand your human father

> If we could read the secret history of our enemies, we should find in each man's life sorrow and suffering enough to disarm all hostility.
>
> Henry Wadsworth Longfellow

In seeking to understand our imperfect human father, we must consider several things:

1. *We live in a fallen world.* Adam and Eve made a sinful choice that affected and changed the entire created world. It filled perfect and beautiful gardens with weeds and thorns. It severed humanity's fellowship/relationship with Creator God. Fortunately, our fellowship has been redeemed and restored through the death and resurrection of Jesus Christ. But we now live in a "lost paradise" (see Gen. 3).

Just consider the cost of our world's fallenness in the last one hundred years alone. We've experienced two World Wars, a holocaust in Europe, genocide in Cambodia, massacre in Rwanda, and untold horrors in the Sudan, Sierra Leone, the two Congos, Northern Ireland, the Middle East, Iran, Iraq . . . the list is endless. This was not the way God created the world. He finished his spectacular creation, looked over what he had done, and proclaimed it "good" (Gen. 1:31)! Surely, wrote Henry David Thoreau, "There is no odor so bad as that which arises from goodness tainted."[1]

How we inwardly yearn for the long-ago goodness of that perfect Garden—a world that knew no bloodshed or hatred or apartheid—a world untainted. How hard it is to live in a world where people can be spiteful and calculating, deceitful and abusive. But live in it we do. And women like Alexandra and Bethany, Joyce and Amy, Catherine and Gayle, Faye, Priscilla, Karen, and Lucy are reared by imperfect fathers who often devastate their young lives, destroy their potential futures, and distort their view of God.

2. *Our human fathers are a product of this fallen world.* Much of who your father is/was came from the teachings of his parents—his larger famil-

ial background—and how these people and other influencers in his life affected him. He is also a product of his environment.

I never learned much about my dad's background and family. They lived in California—quite a distance away from us. Daddy didn't talk much about them. I made one trip to visit them long after I was grown, married, and raising high school-aged children. They were delightful. They showed me family photos and answered most all my questions about Daddy's childhood. Although my dad left home at a young age—he joined the military during World War II at age fifteen—he was greatly loved by his mother, sister, and brother.

Did your father grow up with Christian parents? Did he receive necessary love and kindness as a baby? Was he provided for or was he deprived? Did he have both a mother and a father? If so, how did his parents relate to each other? Did they have a strong marriage or did he endure his parent's divorce, separation, or abandonment? Did he grow up in a Christ-centered environment—home, school, church, neighborhood? All these things can determine your father's personality and viewpoints. For instance, if your father was abused as a child by his father, he most likely grew up to abuse his own children. If your father was reared in an atheistic or secular home, he might be inclined to continue his "belief and value system" in your home. Sins of the fathers are most likely passed onto their children—generation to generation. And unless something or someone intervenes and stops the tragic cycle, these destructive patterns of living and relating to others will continue.

"The things that happen to us very early in life will shape the way we live out the rest of our years. Even if they live to be 120, most people will be following the life-style that was built into them by the time they were four or five years old."[2]

Of course, human beings don't have to stay the way they are. For instance, if your father grew up in an impoverished situation, he might have pursued an education that moved him away from that environment and changed the course of his life. Or if your father grew up as a non-Christian, he might have made the decision to turn to Christ, to embrace Christianity, and to allow the Holy Spirit to give him new perspective, new purpose, and new life. "Going with the flow," so to speak, and living out one's entire life in the "groove" already dug, however, proves the easier way. The life-road has already been cut and paved. The person just puts his feet on the paved path and unconsciously walks through life as his parents and environment conditioned him.

And, as we all know, when a child's feet have been placed on the wrong road, especially one without Christ, the life he leads might be disastrous and detrimental to others. You might have sustained the blunt force of his faulty learned habits and bad training.

Finding one's own way into rightness and truth and Christ's purpose means stepping off the familiar path, and choosing the road less traveled. It's the harder route—the one few people take. Your father was perhaps too weak or passive or afraid to step off the road and make the choice to live a life different from what was familiar.

3. *You need to know that you are not responsible for your father's faulty temperament or harsh personality or underprivileged background.* You are also not to blame for his health problems, financial problems, alcoholism or drug addiction, or behavior problems. Even a grown daughter cannot control her father's choices, nor how other people respond to him. You will not be held accountable for his inappropriate or unwise actions. If you are trying to "parent" your dad, or to change him and his undesirable ways, stop. It won't work. He alone must change his thinking, his attitude, and his behavior. Don't take that huge responsibility onto your shoulders. Catherine isn't responsible for her father's sexual abuse. Neither is Alexandra to blame for her father's hateful attitude and harsh control. Priscilla should not feel guilty because her deadbeat dad abandoned her family. Neither should Karen—or Kelly Osbourne, MacKenzie Phillips, or Drew Barrymore—take the blame for her father's drug/alcohol abuse.

Just as you can't make your irresponsible father into a respectable and responsible gentlemen, neither must you take the blame for his health problems, financial bankruptcies, divorce, or failures. You cannot control what other people do, whether they be your next-door neighbor, a fellow church member, or your own flesh-and-blood father. You can pray for him, try to advise him, make wise suggestions, but that is all.

4. *Your father may have done the best job he could do in parenting you, but didn't possess the skills necessary to be a good father.* He may have severely hurt you, but he might not have hurt you intentionally.

"Who were your parents? Imperfect humans like you and me. They had their own problems with life and were faced with their own childhood memories. The social and cultural forces of their time affected them, and their own marriage relationship had its effect as well.... You were hurt as a child, in most cases, not because your parents really intended to hurt you, but because they did not know better."[3]

As a grown woman, take a moment and examine the early life of your father. Imagine the difference between a dad who grew up suffering imprisonment in a German concentration camp during World War II, and a dad whose last name was Rockefeller.

If your father barely survived the Great Depression or, as a child, had inadequate clothes and shelter and little to eat, his ideals about spending and saving money may be quite different from a father who, as a boy, had plenty to eat, nice clothes to wear, and lived in a big, comfortable house.

If your father had two parents who fussed and fought, who lived like enemies instead of partners, and who betrayed and deceived each other, he may have functioned the same way in his own marriage. The type of marriage his parents modeled for him taught him that was "normal."

If your father received no love or affection from his parents, he may not have known how to give and receive love and affection. A father can give only what he knows. He may not have had a "file" in his "computer bank" that had "love" programmed into it. One cannot "pull up and open" what one never possessed.

If your father grew up with no self-esteem or with a damaged self-confidence, he might have become a workaholic who allowed work to fill the empty hole in his heart. A man usually works for different reasons than a woman. While a woman might work primarily for income, "A man does use his work to build his identity. He uses his work to express who he is ... work also gives a man a purpose for his life."[4] Not that that justifies workaholism or family neglect, but it does help an ignored grown daughter better understand why her father worked all the time.

I am not making excuses for fathers who control, overparent, abandon, or abuse their daughters. But I am suggesting that we, as adult daughters of imperfect parents, seek understanding into why our parent was like he was and did what he did.

If you've suffered under an unbearable father, know that you have several options. You can:

- *Pray for him.* Pray that God will change him and bring him closer to Christ and to his family. God is the ultimate Parent. Only he can change a person's heart and mind and purpose.
- *Separate yourself.* Adulthood gives us options to physically move away from our families.

- *Learn from his mistakes.* By seeking to understand your father's flaws, you can study yourself and your own human flaws. Then you can make some concrete changes in your own life to avoid repeating your parent's imperfections.
- *Consider his weaknesses*, investigate the painful impact they've had on your entire life, and *then choose to forgive him and move ahead.* (Tomorrow we'll examine what it means to forgive your father, and how your forgiveness will set you free from hate and bitterness.)

Let me leave you today with an important thought. It involves what we've already talked about through the pages of this book. It involves uprooting your garden's poison ivy—the harmful plants planted by a flawed human father, and replanting healing herbs offered to you by your perfect heavenly Father. Know that: "You have a choice between being bound by your parents' failures and deficiencies or accepting your past and moving on with your life. You can choose to be responsible for how you feel and respond positively to life, or you can choose to blame your parents for your problems and thus perpetuate their influence in your life. You can choose to live in the past and let the past determine who you are today, or you can choose to learn from the past but live in the present."[5]

In understanding your father and yourself, you will find healing.

Daily Sunlight

Your Personal Time to Grow:

Throughout Ecclesiastes, the author searches for understanding. Have you also searched to understand life, faith, love, your father? If so, explain. What have you found?

_____

_____

_____

_____

[If time allows] Research the early life of your father, and his father, if possible. (You might talk with other living relatives who knew your father and his family, etc.) Then write down your findings. What did you discover? What are some of the positive influences in his life? Negative influences? What did you learn that better helps you to understand his attitude, thinking, opinions, beliefs, behavior, character traits, etc.?

[If time is limited, do this exercise instead] Make some quiet time, and talk to God. Ask him to continue to give you understanding into the background of your father. Ask him to help your father, to bless him, and to bring him close to Christ.

Your Personal Prayer:

Father, thank you for these thoughts about my father as I try to better understand him and his behavior. I can see now that my father is the product of many things—parentage, siblings, inherited genetics, outside relationships, birth order, and other things I will never know. I pray that you will help me to love him, even if I never understand all the whys and whats and hows of his life. Father, please help my dad. Draw near to him. Bless him. Show me how to honor him even though, in many ways, he has dishonored me. I pray all these things in Jesus' precious name, amen.

Week 6: A Time to Heal, A Time for Peace

Day 2: A time to mend — choosing to forgive your flawed father

> Bear with each other and forgive whatever grievances you may have
> against one another. Forgive as the Lord forgave you.
>
> Paul in Colossians 3:13

In Colossians 3:12–17, the apostle Paul tells Christians how to live and relate to other people. He tells us to treat others with compassion and kindness, humility and gentleness, patience and love. He asks that we come together in unity and allow Christ's peace to rule our hearts. He also admonishes us to be thankful to God, to worship with grateful singing, and to work as if we are doing everything for Jesus.

It's a beautiful passage of Scripture which basically springs from this truth: no matter who we are in this life, no matter what we do, where we come from, the size of our savings account, the color of our skin, or our ancestral background, we each have a place in Christ's love (v. 11).

But perhaps my favorite part of the passage is Paul's instruction about forgiveness. He writes: "Bear with each other and forgive whatever grievances you may have against one another. Forgive as the Lord forgave you" (v. 13).

Let's look at this verse as it applies to forgiving a father who hurt you.

Bear with each other. To bear your father's faults means to put up with him even though you find his words and actions hard to stomach. A child, for instance, has little choice but to accept her father and tolerate his weaknesses and poor character traits. This is where understanding comes into a relationship. An adult child might be able to examine her father's background (as we discussed in Day 1), figure out why he acts in a particular way, and better understand and accept his shortcomings. Then she can more readily and eagerly forgive him.

And forgive. To forgive your father means that, even though you may desire revenge and retaliation, you choose to pardon him. In doing so, you do not excuse or condone his acts toward you. But you face his flaws, claim that they did indeed cause you pain, and then withdraw blame. You "let him off the hook." You mark his debt "paid." You hold no more grudges, no more bitterness, against him.

Whatever grievances you may have against [him]. "Whatever grievances" covers a lot of ground in the arena of forgiveness. Does it mean that Catherine can forgive her sexually abusive father? Does it mean that Amy can forgive her dad who "just wasn't there" for her? That Gayle can forgive her father's caustic criticism? That Faye can forgive her father's undependability? That Karen can forgive her drug-addicted dad? Yes, it does. It means that you can choose to forgive "whatever grievances" you hold against your father, no matter what they are. It may not be easy to forgive him, and it might take a long time. Forgiveness doesn't happen in an instant. It is often a tedious and grueling process. But it is possible.

Forgive as the Lord forgave you. How did the Lord forgive us? God's Word tells us we have all sinned (Rom. 3:23) and that we all need forgiveness to be made right with him again (10:9–10). John 3:16 assures us that God has made a way for us to be forgiven and to receive eternal life and reconciliation with our heavenly Father. Because we have been forgiven so much, God expects us to forgive those who also need forgiveness (Col. 3:13). An important part of living a Christlike life is to choose forgiveness over hatred, revenge, retaliation, and bitterness.

Yesterday we looked at what it means to seek to understand your flawed father. After we've sought understanding, the next step is to forgive him for the complications, heartache, and struggles he has caused us. Some fathers are harder to forgive than others. For instance, it will probably be easier for Faye to forgive her dad's undependability than for Catherine to forgive her father's ugly sexual abuse. But, no matter what the circumstances or abuses, forgiveness is necessary for healing. (If you have a problem forgiving your father [or anyone else], for any reason, I urge you to read *Cultivating a Forgiving Heart: Forgiveness Frees You to Flourish*, another book in the "Secrets of Soul Gardening" series. Many myths keep us from forgiving those who hurt us. In *Cultivating a Forgiving Heart*, I list those myths and explain how forgiveness benefits the forgiver, not necessarily the one who needs the forgiveness. I also explain how a woman can forgive an offender regardless of the offense.)

"You may feel sad, angry or even bitter that your family has contributed so much to your problems and struggles as an adult. I urge you not to look backward in anger, but to look forward in hope. You cannot change the past or any of the behavior which you wish could be different. Focus your energies on forgiving family members for the past and on building positive, healthy relationships for the future."[6]

What is forgiveness? "Forgiving the offender means you cancel the debt. You release the person from the payment. You give the miracle of pardon and set the offender free from the owed debt. Mercy given, grace granted—it's a mysterious process, one that goes against our human instincts. The person certainly doesn't deserve your forgiveness, but you can give your forgiveness anyway."[7]

Does forgiveness mean reconciliation? Must you restore a relationship with your forgiven father? Not necessarily. Of course, reconciliation is the ideal outcome in your relationship with your father. But forgiveness can happen, and be genuine and complete, even if you decide reconciliation isn't in your best interest. (I will not elaborate on the topic of reconciliation here because I have covered it in detail in *Cultivating a Forgiving Heart*.)

As I've already said, genuine forgiveness seldom happens overnight. But the process of choosing to forgive a father who has hurt you takes only a second to begin. You must do it in order to find Christ's healing and peace. You are the one who will most benefit from forgiving your father. Don't allow the weeds of bitterness to grow in your garden any longer. Pull them up by the roots. Get rid of them. They take up valuable soil space you can use to grow productive, fruit-producing plants!

Daily Sunlight

Your Personal Time to Grow:

Read Ecclesiastes 12:13, in which Solomon offers two final suggestions for living a fruitful life. What are they? What will taking his recommendations do for your own life?

_____

_____

_____

_____

Read Ephesians 4:31–32—Paul's words about bitterness, rage, anger, brawling and slander, which are usually the by-products of an unforgiving heart. Consider your father and his behavior toward you. What do you find the most difficult thing to forgive?

_____

_____

_____

_____

How will forgiving your father release you from the bondage of bitterness?

_____

_____

_____

_____

If you are ready to make a decision, choose to forgive your father for everything he did to you that needs your forgiveness. Know that this is the first step in the long journey to completely forgive him, but it is the most important decision you can make.

Your Personal Prayer:

Father, my dad horribly mistreated me. I find it difficult to forgive him for what he has done. I'd rather blame him for his actions, hold them against him, forget all about his words and deeds, and move ahead. But I know that if I don't stop to examine his faults and forgive him, then I'll be burdened with hate and bitterness for the rest of my life. I don't want to live a life imprisoned by unforgiveness, resentment, and hostility. I want to find healing from my painful childhood. I want to live my life in Christ and in his offered peace. I know that I will only experience this peace if I forgive my father's faults. As hard as it is to do, I want to make the decision right now to forgive him. I don't excuse what he did; neither do I condone it. But I have chosen to completely forgive him. Help me, Father, as I embark upon this difficult journey toward complete forgiveness and freedom. In the name of your Son, amen.

Week 6: A Time to Heal, A Time for Peace

Day 3: A time to build—adding new herbs to your garden

> But the fruit of the Spirit is love, joy, peace, patience, kindness, goodness, faithfulness, gentleness and self-control.
>
> Paul in Galatians 5:22–23

Over the past two days, you have examined your father's background and sought to understand why he acts and reacts like he does to you, your family, and others. You may have also decided to forgive your father for all the hurt and pain he has caused you. Let's stop for a moment, visit your imaginary garden, and decide what to do next.

In your mind, "look" at your newly planted garden. Do you see the productive plants and healing herbs that now fill the soil's holes where poison ivy and weeds once grew? You have planted your garden well. Your garden's new seedlings are beginning to take root and grow. Tomorrow we will see how each new plant must be cared for and nurtured. Today, however, we will decide what other seedlings we will choose to plant in our new garden.

Scripture encourages believers in Christ to plant good seeds that will produce good fruit—a bountiful harvest. Fortunately, we don't have to guess what seeds to include in our new gardens. In Galatians 5:22, the apostle Paul gives us a list. Let's look closely at the "good seeds" Paul recommends, and examine what God's Word says about each one:

Love. God is love. We are to love God and love each other. What is love? Love is something we *do*, not necessarily something we *feel*. Our feelings can come and go and change. Christ's love reaches out and ministers to others. We are called to love even those who are unlovable. Through active caring love, believers show the world they are Christ's disciples.

Joy. As believers in Christ, we are promised God's joy even when we suffer hardships and pain. Joy is different than human happiness. Happiness depends on what is happening. Joy depends on the love and forgiveness, acceptance and salvation Christ gives us, his daughters. (Read Psalm 100 to learn how we can respond to God with joy.)

Peace. Although we live in a time where peace is rare, God offers us his peace. God's peace is not dependent on our circumstances, but on our relationship with Christ. The world cannot understand this heartfelt peace that Christians possess. It baffles them. Peace is knowing in whom you believe, why you were born, your purpose on earth, and your destination in heaven when you leave this earth. (Read Jesus' promise about peace in John 14:27.)

Patience. Patience proves a rare quality among people, even Christians, in our fast-paced, instant society. Yet Christ commands it. In dealing with others, the writer of Proverbs states: "A man's wisdom gives him patience; it is to his glory to overlook an offense" (Prov. 19:11). The gift of patience gives "a gentle answer [that] turns away wrath, but a harsh word [and perhaps an *impatient* word?] stirs up anger" (15:1). Paul urges believers to "clothe" themselves with patience (Col. 3:12; see also 1:11).

Goodness. Jesus himself sets the example of showing goodness to those he met. He fed the hungry, healed the sick, answered theological questions, took little children onto his lap and blessed them. Or consider just a few of the early Christians mentioned in Acts: *Philip* showed goodness when he interrupted his travels and went out of his way to explain Old Testament Scripture to the Ethiopian eunuch (Acts 8:26–40). *Ananias* showed goodness when he risked life and limb to nurse Paul after the greatly feared Christian killer was converted (9:1–19).

Faithfulness. Surely, the personification of "faithfulness" would be Mary Magdalene. When Jesus cast out seven demons that indwelled Mary's body (Luke 8:2), Mary became one of Jesus' most faithful followers. She personally helped support Jesus' ministry (8:1–3); she followed him to the cross in the midst of great danger (Matt. 27:56; Mark 15:40; John 19:25); and she followed him to his grave (Matt. 27:61; Mark 15:47). Maybe because of Mary's faithfulness, Jesus allowed her to be the first eyewitness of his resurrection (Matt. 28:1–10; Mark 16:1–9; Luke 24:1–12).

Gentleness. Gentleness is an innate calmness and tenderness. God's love requires and equips us to become tender in a tough world. Scripture tells us that Christ has a gentle heart (Matt. 11:29; also see 2 Cor. 10:1, where Paul proclaims Christ's gentleness). In Philippians 4:5, Paul writes, "Let your gentleness be evident to all." In Colossians 3:12, he urges believers to put on gentleness like clothing and wear it. He charges young Timothy to "pursue righteousness, godliness, faith, love, endurance and gentleness" (1 Tim. 6:11).

Self-control. "Let us be alert and self-controlled," Paul urges the Thessalonians, "putting on faith and love as a breastplate, and the hope of salvation as a helmet" (1 Thess. 5:6, 8). Think of these synonyms: self-discipline, restraint, strength of mind. The opposite of self-control is self-indulgence—a flaw no Christian should give in to.

Why have I suggested to plant small plants or seedlings instead of large, mature plants? Because a seedling represents a start, a small beginning. Producing fruit can't happen overnight. But with consistent nurture, the seedling sprouts, roots grow deep, stems grow strong, and then a mature plant produces flower and fruit.

The seedling is like our spiritual growth. Spiritual growth always starts small, with the single decision to follow Christ. After the seedling of salvation is planted, then we must nurture it with prayer, Bible study, quiet meditation, Christian fellowship, corporate and personal worship, and so on. The Spirit guides our spiritual growth, as we sink deep roots into God's Word. When we mature in our faith, we are ready to produce eternal fruit.

Daily Sunlight

Your Personal Time to Grow:

Reread Galatians 5:22–23. Now read *at least one* Scripture for each of the fruit and write a brief thought about each:

Love (1 Cor. 13:1–4)

_____

Joy (Ps. 100)

_____

Peace (John 14:27)

_____

Patience (Prov. 19:11; 15:1; James 1:2–5)

_____

Goodness (Acts 8:26–40; 9:1–19; 9:36–39)

_____

Faithfulness (Matt. 27:56; Mark 15:47; 16:1–9)

_____

Gentleness (Matt. 11:29; 2 Cor. 10:1; Phil. 4:5)

_____

Self-control (1 Thess. 5:6, 8)

_____

From this list of "fruit of the Spirit" seedlings, note, in order of their importance to you, those that you most want to plant in your new garden (incorporate in your life) and explain why.

_____

_____

_____

_____

_____

Choose some other seedlings to plant too. What other godly attributes (hospitality, generosity, kindness, helpfulness, self-giving nurture, etc.) would you most like to include in your life?

_____

_____

_____

_____

Plant your chosen seedlings. Using your imagination, envision yourself kneeling in your garden soil, digging a small hole, and placing your seedling into it—a young plant that will grow, mature, and produce the Spirit's fruit—joy, peace, patience, goodness, faithfulness, gentleness, self-control, and other virtues. Cover the tiny roots and base of each planted seedling with soil, sprinkle with water, and fertilize.

Your Personal Prayer:

Father, please help me to become the Christlike woman that you want me to be. I am trying to incorporate love, joy, peace, patience, goodness, faithfulness, gentleness, and self-control into my everyday life. I pray that I can keep these good, productive "plants" growing, thriving, and producing in my new garden. In Jesus' name, amen.

Week 6: A Time to Heal, A Time for Peace

Day 4: A time to love—nurturing your garden's new plants

> You can plant seeds and then water, fertilize, and cultivate a field, but it is the Lord who turns seeds into a harvest.
>
> Charles Stanley, *Finding Peace*

You have chosen good seedlings to plant in your new garden, seedlings that represent a new direction for you, your faith, and your family. They are planted, watered, and fertilized. Your new garden is complete. Now the growth is up to the Master Gardener.

Nurturing your faith to the point of bearing fruit involves surrender to your heavenly Father as well as your own tender care, love, and protection. Here are the Spirit's gardening tools:

- Prayer
- Bible study
- Worship
- Christian friends
- Quiet
- Service
- Abiding in Christ

Let's look at each one individually:

Prayer. Prayer is simply communicating and communing with your heavenly Father, both speaking to God and listening to God speak to you. God's gift of prayer provides intimacy with the Father, "Abba." Jesus himself spent much time communicating and communing with the Father in prayer. Through prayer, God strengthens and comforts us, encourages and supports us. Through prayer, we learn his will for our lives. Find a special prayer "closet" where you can make an appointment each day with the Lord and spend time with him. (To learn how to pray during difficult times, read my book *Tilling the Soul: Prayer Penetrates Your Pain*, also in the "Secrets of Soul Gardening" series.)

Bible study. God inspired the Bible's authors to write his Word. The Bible reveals God through Jesus Christ, shows us the way to salvation in him, and serves as a guidebook to tell us how to live the Christian life. When we read and study Scripture, we discover and learn to appreciate our rich historical Christian roots. God's Word is daily nourishment for our soul.

Worship. Worship, both personal and in a body of believers, is an important part of spiritual growth. Worship includes reading and hearing God's Word, as well as praying, singing, and fellowshiping as a believing Christian community.

Christian friends. Fellow believers can keep us growing in the faith as they pray for us, encourage us, listen to us when we hurt, and rejoice with us when we rejoice. Rich is the woman who has one good Christian friend who genuinely loves her.

Quiet. Every Christian needs time alone to quietly think, meditate, ponder, and reflect on faith, family, friends, and future. Restful quiet time refreshes the inner woman. It restores her soul. (To learn how to rest in the Lord, and find quiet time in a chaotic, busy society, I would encourage you to read my book *Come to the Quiet: The Secrets of Solitude and Rest.*)

Service. The world's hurting women need you. Service to others in the name of Christ—loving them with God's heart and reaching out to them with God's hands—is like the sunshine and gentle rain that nourishes growing plants. We grow spiritually when we follow Christ's example and minister to others in his name.

Abiding in Christ. "I am the vine; you are the branches. If you remain in me and I in you, you will bear much fruit; apart from me you can do nothing. . . . This is to my Father's glory, that you bear much fruit, showing yourselves to be my disciples. . . . You did not choose me, but I chose you and appointed you so that you might go and bear fruit—fruit that will last" (John 15:5, 8, 16 TNIV). Depend on the Gardener, and stay close to him.

Daily Sunlight

Your Personal Time to Grow:

Does Solomon's advice in the book of Ecclesiastes encourage or discourage you? Explain. Do you agree with his statements or disagree, and why?

_____

_____

_____

_____

_____

In John 15:7, Jesus encourages his followers to bring their requests to him, and then he promises to grant those requests. When you consider your relationship with your father, what request would you like Jesus to grant for you?

_____

_____

_____

In John 15:13–14, Jesus describes the difference between a servant and a friend, and calls his followers _friends_. What does the word _friend_ mean to you? Do you think of Christ as your friend? Why or why not?

_____

_____

_____

Plan a time when you can daily pray, study Scripture, quietly rest, and reflect. Choose a quiet place in your house, office, garden, etc., where you can "meet" with God for personal worship.

Your Personal Prayer:

Father, thank you for planting within me your seed of salvation and faith. I pray that I may trust you completely in my growth as a Christian woman. I want to abide in you like a branch abides in the vine. Thank you, Father, for your gift of prayer, for your precious Word, for the ability you give your daughters to think and reflect, for Christian friends, for your church and the beauty of worship, for the privilege to trust you completely, and for the opportunity to serve others in your name. I want to grow and mature and bear fruit, Father—fruit that will last. In Jesus' name, amen.

Day 5: A time to laugh and dance—experiencing the Gardener's joy

> God designed us to have this intimate relationship with Himself. He knew that out of this intimacy of relationship we could receive His gift to all who follow Him—a deep, lasting, abiding peace that only He can provide to the human heart.
>
> Charles Stanley, *Finding Peace*

For the past six weeks, you and I have walked together through your garden. You have taken time to examine the events of your childhood, and select the good times with your human father you want to keep and treasure. You've discovered that all human fathers are flawed in some way, and that the only perfect father is God the Father. After reflecting on your father's faults—all those things he did that hurt you in some way—you've decided to throw away and uproot those poisonous plants that still grow in your life-garden.

Through Scripture, you've learned that your human father was only a caretaker for your childhood and adolescence, and that your true and eternal Father is your Father in heaven. You've embraced God's fatherly gifts that he offers to you through his Son, Jesus. You've seen that the same soil that grows poison ivy can also grow healing herbs. You've planted his loving and faith-producing seedlings. You are studying his Word and allowing your Father to nurture you, to grow you up strong and mature so that you can produce fruit for him.

You've sought understanding into your human father's background, and you've tried to figure out why he related to you as he did. Perhaps you've chosen to forgive your flawed father, letting go of all your hurt, resentments, anger, and bitterness. You may have pardoned your dad and released him from the debt of pain and suffering he caused you.

Now, as you look to your heavenly Father for your future spiritual growth, let me suggest some last things that must be done in order for you to laugh, dance, and experience the good Gardener's joy:

Embrace your special status as a daughter of your heavenly Father. He has a purpose for you, a reason for your life. Listen to the Lord's words to his prophet Jeremiah. They are words for you today. "'For I know the plans I have for you,' declares the LORD, 'plans to prosper you and not to harm you, plans to give you hope and a future. Then you will call upon me and come and pray to me, and I will listen to you. You will seek me and find me when you seek me with all your heart'" (Jer. 29:11–13).

Trust your heavenly Father completely. You were created "to know God, to return God's love, and to enjoy communion with God. That's the meaning of life," writes Chuck Colson.[8] Peace comes from trusting God, for he created you and you belong to him. St. Augustine stated this truth in a beautiful way: "Thou hast made us for thyself," he wrote, "and our heart has no rest till it comes to Thee."[9] Your peace rests in your ability to completely trust your heavenly Father. Scripture promises, "You [God] will keep in perfect peace those whose minds are steadfast, because they trust in you" (Isa. 26:3 TNIV).

Let go of the past and its pain, and believe in the future. Lloyd Ogilvie gives good advice to believers when he writes: "The sure sign that we have an authentic relationship with God is that we believe more in the future than in the past. The past can be neither a source of confidence nor a condemnation. God graciously divided our life into days and years so that we could let go of yesterdays and anticipate our tomorrows. For the past mistakes, He offers forgiveness and an ability to forget. For our tomorrows, He gives us the gift of expectation and excitement."[10]

As you nurture your new plants, nurture yourself. How can you nurture yourself as you grow in faith to maturity?

1. *Forgive yourself* for your life's wrongdoings. God has already forgiven you, his cleansed daughter. Let go of those debts you hold against yourself. Without self-forgiveness, there is no peace.
2. *Accept yourself* even though you know well your own flaws. God accepts you just as you are. Stop striving for perfection, and start aiming to do your best. Perfection cannot be achieved in this life. Don't allow other people to determine who you are and what you are worth. That's your Father's job. "God has to be the source of your self-esteem and how you view yourself as a woman. Looking to another human being, or to a cultural movement . . . for your inner peace and sense of worth will always result in disappointment."[11]

3. *Affirm and encourage yourself.* You can become your worst critic when your inner voice constantly tells you that: you aren't good enough, you'll never accomplish anything, you can't do anything right, and so on. Speak kindly to yourself as you would speak to a friend. Realize your strengths, and affirm who you are in Christ. Don't allow feelings of self-doubt to immobilize you. "Instead of being immobilized by the challenges in your life, use anxiety as a stimulus to growth. Rather than hoping that someone else will find the right words to comfort and encourage you, you can be that person yourself . . . giving yourself at least the same understanding you would give your closest friend."[12]

4. *Allow God to "refather" you, to "reparent" you.* "God powerfully met me as a broken and lost twenty-year-old woman who needed a father's touch," writes Dee Clark (the daughter of an emotionally distant dad you met in Day 3 of Week 2). "God has a way of healing the brokenhearted and fixing the mistakes and neglect of others."[13]

I've found several Scriptures that state with clarity the peace that God through Christ offers you:

God's name is "peace," *Yahweh-Shalom*: "The Lord is peace" (Judg. 6:24).

Jesus promises: "Peace I leave with you; my peace I give you. I do not give to you as the world gives. Do not let your hearts be troubled and do not be afraid" (John 14:27).

"I have told you these things," Jesus says, "so that in me you may have peace. In this world you will have trouble. But take heart! I have overcome the world" (John 16:33).

Paul ends his letter to the Romans with this blessing and promise of peace. May I also end "my letter" to you with these words: "May the God of hope fill you with all joy and peace as you trust in him, so that you may overflow with hope by the power of the Holy Spirit" (Rom. 15:13).

In closing, may I suggest that, in your journey, you seek out good Christian friends who will love, nurture, and encourage you. Robert S. McGee writes: "Persons who have received poor parental modeling need new models—loving Christian friends—to help them experience the love and grace of God. Through His body of believers God often provides us with models of His love, so that our perception of His character slowly can be reshaped into one that is more accurate. This results in a healthier relationship with Him. Then our deep emotional, spiritual, and relational wounds can begin to heal, and we more fully can experience God's unconditional love."[14]

While you are making new friends, don't forget old friends. Reestablish communication and friendships with those good, nurturing Christian friends you've known in the past. Friends make our journey less difficult and more enjoyable. Christian friends can give us strength and encouragement. Don't allow distance or relocation or busyness to disconnect you from those you love. Get back in touch with them. Remember—you can't make "old friends," and some of them are like precious gold!

Daily Sunlight

Your Personal Time to Grow:

What does the writer of Ecclesiastes teach you about life today? Do his words fill you with heaviness and confusion or joy and peace? Why?

_____

_____

_____

_____

_____

The Psalms show us many different ways to trust God. Read the following Scriptures and answer the questions:

Psalm 11: The psalmist trusted God to judge evil men, because he knew God was in control. Have you given God control of your life? Are you holding back anything from him that he alone needs to control?

_____

_____

_____

Psalm 27: The psalmist trusted God to keep him secure in his arms even during difficult times. During your difficult times, how do you find security in God's arms, and in God's promises?

_____

_____

Psalm 63: The psalmist trusted God to stay close to him and keep him safe. In what ways do you stay close to God? Do you trust God to keep you safe? How? (Give some examples of times you trusted God when you faced danger.)

_____

_____

_____

_____

Psalm 139: The psalmist trusted God and praised him. What is your favorite way to praise God? Why is praise important to your personal worship time?

_____

_____

Now let's focus on one final issue concerning both your father and your ongoing spiritual growth.

What should you do with the hurtful memories that you collected in your childhood from painful events involving your father? How do you rid your mind of bad memories that can now interfere with your daily life, family, career, and worship? Here are some suggestions:

Ask the Holy Spirit to bring to your mind all those memories you need to deal with—all those memories you need to put out of your mind and life.

As the Holy Spirit brings each memory to your mind, write it down. Record everything you remember about the situation. Describe your surroundings at the time.

Ask yourself: why did my dad, and this experience with him, cause me such pain? Record your answer.

Envision yourself stepping into your father's shoes at the time of the painful incident. Seek to understand why he did or said hurtful things to you.

Pray that God will help you to forgive him.

Make a conscious choice to forgive him as you recall, and reflect upon, each painful memory the Holy Spirit brings to your mind. It often helps to imagine yourself talking directly to your father. Tell him: "Dad, you hurt me when _____. I felt _____ when you said or did that particular thing. Dad, I forgive you for _____."

After you imagine telling your dad you forgive him, envision his response to you in this way: "_____ (the name he called you), I am sorry for _____ (what he did), and I ask your forgiveness. Thank you for your forgiveness."

Ask God to allow you to remove the painful power of the memory. You probably won't forget what happened to you, but you can be freed from the destructive power the memories have over you.

At times, you might feel sad that your childhood was marred by a father who failed to love you, or who ignored or abused you. When that sadness surfaces, when you ache for the kind, loving human father you never had, how should you deal with those feelings? How can you find healing? Here are some suggestions:

Ask Christ to enter into your thoughts, give you healing for your feelings, and allow you to experience further peace. (Paul writes that the believer should take every thought captive to Christ. See 2 Cor. 10:5.)

Visualize God standing beside you. Listen to his words as he tells you: "You are my beloved daughter, and I am well pleased with you." (The Father said these words to his Son, Jesus, after Jesus had been baptized. See Matt. 3:17.)

Find a photograph of yourself as a child. Sit down in a quiet place where you'll not be interrupted. Look at the child in the picture. Study her. Experience the pain she might have felt at the moment the photo was taken.

Visualize that child in the photograph walking up to you, extending her hand, and taking your hand.

Imagine yourself picking up that little girl, and putting her on your lap. Tell her that she is God's daughter, and that he loves her so much that he gave his only Son, Jesus, to die on a cross so that she might live with him forever. Tell her that she is like a little seedling in God's garden, and that her heavenly Father will take care of her. Remind her of God's presence in her life, and his plan for her life.

Embrace and nurture her. Tell her not to fear the future for God, her heavenly Father, is in control. Hold her in your lap until she becomes calm and peaceful. Talk to her, sing to her, and then pray with her.

As you hold the child you were, imagine that Jesus is standing next to you. He is smiling as you speak to your inner child, and as you comfort her, sing to her, and pray with her.

Ask Jesus to sit down with you, put his hands on you both, and bless you with his joy and peace.

Finally (as you, your inner child, and Jesus sit down together in your imagination), visualize Jesus opening your favorite Bible to Philippians 4:8–9, and reading this Scripture aloud: "Whatever is true, whatever is noble, whatever is right, whatever is pure, whatever is lovely, whatever is admirable— if anything is excellent or praiseworthy—think about such things. Whatever you have learned or received or heard from me, or seen in me—put it into practice. And the God of peace will be with you."

Remember, by doing this simple exercise, you are bringing healing to your inner child—the little girl whose heart was broken and whose spirit was crushed by someone (her father) she desperately wanted to love, trust, and look up to with respect, admiration, and deep friendship. In this way, you can "reparent" yourself and find healing. Whenever you feel the need, repeat this exercise.

[Note: You may want to seek out the help of a Christian counselor to help you deal with your painful memories.]

Your Personal Prayer:

Father, thank you for the promise in your Word that tells me: "What this means is that those who become Christians become new persons. They are not the same anymore, for the old life is gone. A new life has begun!" (2 Cor. 5:17 NLT). I am ready to fully embark upon that new life! The old has truly gone—and with it all the pain I suffered at the hands of my father. And the new has come—I have discovered that you are my ultimate Father, my perfect Parent, and I love you. I pray that you will help me grow to maturity and produce fruit for you and your kingdom. Thank you for your hope, joy, and peace! In Jesus' name I pray, amen.

*"A Time to Heal,
A Time for Peace"*

Growing Together in God's Word:

1. Discuss together the meaning of Ecclesiastes. In a sentence or two, state your own philosophy or understanding of life and faith.

   _____

   _____

2. Read 2 Timothy 1:5. (Paul sees in Timothy a "sincere faith.") As a Christian, from whom did you receive "a sincere faith"? Who brought you to a saving knowledge of Christ?

   _____

3. Paul gives good advice in Colossians 3:13. How can taking his advice benefit you, especially as it relates to your father?

   _____

   _____

4. Read John 15:1–17, and then answer these questions:

   a. In your relationship with Christ, how are you like the branch in relationship to Christ as the vine?

   _____

   _____

b. Describe the closeness you feel for Christ. Describe the closeness you would like to experience in Christ.

_____

_____

c. As a "branch," how should you depend on Christ for nourishment, foundation, and growth?

_____

_____

5. In Judges 6:24, Gideon named the altar he built to the Lord "The LORD is peace." (If time permits, read Judges 6.) Discuss: Have you ever experienced this kind of peace? If so, describe it. How did it make you feel? How did God's peace change your life?

_____

_____

6. Allow each group member to give her definition of "peace." How is the peace that Christ offers you different from the peace the world tries to offer you? In what areas of your life today do you see the most need for peace? Explain why.

_____

_____

Group Prayer:

[Pray aloud in unison] Father, we greatly desire the peace that you promise us in your Word. We want your "perfect peace." We know only you can provide the peace that passes all human understanding. Help us to trust you completely. Even if we have not been able to trust our human fathers, show us how to completely trust you, our heavenly Father. Show us how to let go of the past and to believe in the future. Please teach us how to nurture the new plants — the healing herbs — in our replanted gardens. We pray that poison ivy will never grow there again. We want to believe in ourselves as your daughters, and we want to step out in faith and in your

name bear fruit for you. Please, our heavenly Father, fill in those painful gaps left by our human fathers. We have forgiven them, and we have forgiven ourselves for all our wrongdoings. Please father us — each one of us individually — dear Jesus, and equip us to be useful in your kingdom work. Please heal the broken hearts and crushed spirits we've dragged with us from our childhoods. We long to laugh and dance, Father, as we, your daughters, embrace your love, nurture, hope, and peace. In our heavenly Father's name — our true Father — we pray, amen.

Notes

Before You Begin

1. "In 1998 the prestigious *American Journal of Preventative Medicine* published a landmark study by a team of researchers at Kaiser Permanente Medical Care Program working with epidemiologists from the Centers of Disease Control (CDC) in Atlanta. The survey of nearly 20,000 people found that those with 'adverse childhood experiences' were, as adults, far more likely to suffer from cancer, heart disease, chronic lung disorders, and other leading causes of death. . . . Those who had encountered abuse (physical, psychological, or sexual), or were raised in dysfunctional families (with violence, substance abuse, mental illness, or criminal behavior), were far more likely to develop life-threatening illnesses. In fact, an adverse childhood proves to be as powerful a predictor of subsequent illness as smoking. . . . People whose early years are marked by emotional injury are far more likely to have high health risk factors. The study found a strong correlation between childhood adversity and obesity, physical inactivity, and smoking, as well as depression and suicide attempts." In Harold Bloomfield with Philip Goldberg, *Making Peace with Your Past* (New York: HarperCollins, 2000), preface.

2. H. Norman Wright, *Making Peace with Your Past* (Grand Rapids: Baker/Revell, 1985, 2004), 35, my emphasis.

Week 1: A Time to Keep

1. The Pharisees flourished during the last two centuries before Christ and during the first Christian century. Jesus criticized Pharisees for their lack of compassion, for their failure to practice what they preached, and for their contempt for people who could not obey the Law as carefully as they did. Robert S. McGee, *Search for Significance* (Nashville: LifeWay Press, 1992), 66.

2. Gregory E. Lang, *Why a Daughter Needs a Dad* (Nashville: Cumberland House, 2002), n.p.

Week 2: A Time to Throw Away

1. Kenneth O. Gangel and Jeffrey S. Gangel, *Fathering Like the Father* (Grand Rapids: Baker, 2003), 13.

2. Rhonda Harrington Kelley, *Life Lessons from Women in the Bible* (Nashville: LifeWay, 1998), 81.

3. John MacArthur, *What the Bible Says About Parenting* (Nashville: Word Publishing, 2000), 133.

4. Tim Kimmel, *Powerful Personalities* (Colorado Springs: Focus on the Family, 1993), 14.

5. http://www.geocities.com/andrea_w6/otis.html, accessed 8 June 2004.

6. http://www.towson.edu/users/lglass/movies/monroe.htm, accessed 8 June 2004.

7. http://www.crimelibrary.com/notorious_murders/celebrity/marilyn_monroe/2.html?sect=26, accessed 8 June , 2004.

8. http://www.towson.edu/users/lglass/movies/monroe.htm, accessed 8 June 2004.

9. http://ellensplace.net/biomore2.html, accessed 3 June 2004.

10. Kevin Leman, *Women Who Try Too Hard: Breaking the Pleaser Habits* (Grand Rapids: Fleming H. Revell, 1987), 52.

11. Ibid., 55.

12. Charles Sell, "Showing Affection," *Homelife* Magazine, September 2002, 58.

13. Leman, 94.

14. Chap and Dee Clark, *Daughters and Dads: Building a Lasting Relationship* (Colorado Springs: NavPress, 1998), 70.

15. Ibid., 71.

16. Thornton Wilder, *Our Town* (New York: HarperCollins, 1938, 1965, 1985, 1998), 105.

17. Ibid., 107.

18. Clark, 144.

19. Ibid., 128.

20. Kevin Leman, *What a Difference a Daddy Makes* (Nashville: Thomas Nelson, 2000), 52.

21. H. Norman Wright, *Always Daddy's Girl* (Ventura, Calif.: Regal, 1989), 99–100.

22. MacArthur, *What the Bible Says About Parenting*, 141–42.

23. Kevin Leman, *When Your Best Isn't Good Enough* (Grand Rapids: Fleming H. Revell/Baker, 1988), 129.

Week 3: A Time to Uproot

1. http://www.crimelibrary.com/notorious_murders/women/wuornos/2.html?sect=11, accessed 3 June 2004.

2. http://www.crimelibrary.com/notorious_murders/famous/smith/unthinkable_2.html?sect=11, accessed 3 June 2004.

3. Reeni Fenholt, *Integrity of a Father* (Enumclaw, Wash.: WinePress Publishing, 2002), 34.

4. Lewis B. Smedes, *Shame and Grace* (New York: HarperCollins, 1993), 5.

5. Ibid., 9.

6. John Bradshaw, in H. Norman Wright, *Always Daddy's Girl* (Ventura, Calif.: Regal, 1989), 160–61.

7. http://www.crimelibrary.com/notorious_murders/women/folbigg/2.html?sect=11, accessed 3 June 2004.

8. John MacArthur, *What the Bible Says About Parenting* (Nashville: Word Publishing, 2000), 145.

9. *The World Book Encyclopedia*, vol. 4 (Chicago: Field Enterprises Educational Corp., 1963), 16.

10. Normajean Hinders, *Seasons of a Woman's Life* (Nashville: Broadman and Holman, 1994), 178.

11. H. Norman Wright, *Making Peace with Your Past* (Grand Rapids: Baker/Revell, 1985, 2004), 88.

12. http://www.crimelibrary.com/notorious_murders/angels/genene_jones/2.html?sect=11, accessed 3 June 2004.

13. Ken Canfield, http://www.fathers.com/articles/articles.asp?id=121&cat=12, no date given, accessed 6 May 2004.

14. Gary Smalley and John Trent, *The Language of Love* (Pomona, Calif.: Focus on the Family Publishing, 1988), 139.

15. Todd Wilson, http://www.christianitytoday.com/ . . . etter/2003/cmn31003.html, accessed 16 May 2004.

16. Wayne and Joshua Mack, *The Fear Factor* (Tulsa: Hensley Publishing, 2002), 224.

17. http://www.famousnetwork.com/drew_barrymore_biography.htm, accessed 4 June 2004.

18. http://www.abcnews.go.com/onair/2020/2020_991206_phillips_chat.html, accessed 3 June 2004.

19. http://news.bbc.co.uk/go/pr/fr/-/1/hi/entertainment/music/3741461.stm, Published: 2004/05/24 07:46:29 GMT, accessed 3 June 2004.

20. Robert S. McGee gives the definition of a dysfunctional family as "a family in which alcoholism, drug abuse, divorce, absent father or mother, excessive anger, verbal and/or physical abuse exists." In *Search for Significance* (Nashville: LifeWay Press, 1992), 14.

Week 4: A Time to Trust, A Time to Embrace

1. Kevin Leman, *Making Sense of the Men in Your Life* (Nashville: Thomas Nelson, 2000), 90.

2. Kenneth O. Gangel and Jeffrey S. Gangel, *Fathering Like the Father* (Grand Rapids: Baker, 2003), 31.

3. Lewis B. Smedes, *Shame and Grace* (New York: HarperCollins, 1993), 107–8.

4. Charles Stanley, *Finding Peace* (Nashville: Thomas Nelson, 2003), 216.

5. Leman, 92.

6. John Eldredge, *Wild At Heart* (Nashville: Thomas Nelson, 2001), 31.

7. H. Norman Wright, *Making Peace with Your Past* (Grand Rapids: Baker/Fleming H. Revell, 1985, 2004), 109.

8. Chap and Dee Clark, *Daughters and Dads: Building a Lasting Relationship* (Colorado Springs: NavPress, 1998), 79.

9. Ken Hemphill, *Christianity Today*, 22 October 2001, Vol. 45, No. 13, 95.

10. Nancy Leigh DeMoss, *Lies Women Believe* (Chicago: Moody, 2001), 53.

11. Smedes, 6.

Week 5: A Time to Plant

1. T. W. Hunt and Melana Hunt Monroe, *From Heaven's View* (Nashville: Broadman and Holman, 2002), 26.

2. Philip Yancey, *What's So Amazing About Grace?* (Grand Rapids: Zondervan, 1997), 71.

3. Lewis B. Smedes, *Shame and Grace* (New York: HarperCollins, 1993), 109.

4. Neil T. Anderson and Rich Miller, *Freedom from Fear* (Eugene, Ore.: Harvest House, 1999), 174.

5. Ken Canfield, "Dads' Importance to Daughters," http://www.fathers.com/articles.asp?id=468&cat=12, accessed 6 May 2004.

6. http://www.aloe-vera.org/, accessed 19 May 2004.

7. Ken Hemphill, *The Names of God* (Nashville: Broadman and Holman, 2001), 10.

8. In Richard J. Foster and Emilie Griffin, *Spiritual Classics* (San Francisco: HarperSanFrancisco, 2000), 120–22.

9. Ibid., 122–23.

10. H. Norman Wright, *Making Peace with Your Past* (Grand Rapids: Baker/Fleming H. Revell, 1985, 2004), 11.

11. Thaddeus and Erilynne Barnum, *Remember Eve* (DeBary, Fla.: Longwood Communications, 1995), 38.

12. Robert S. McGee, *Search for Significance* (Nashville: LifeWay, 1992), 74.

13. Chap and Dee Clark, *Daughters and Dads* (Colorado Springs: NavPress, 1998), 162.

14. Ibid.

15. http://www.divorceinfo.com/judithwallerstein.htm, accessed 3 June 2004. Judith Wallerstein began her research on the long-term effects of divorce in the early 1970s with 131 children of divorce. She continued to follow those same families as the children matured into adulthood and began families of their own.

16. Walter A. Elwell, ed., *Evangelical Dictionary of Theology* (Grand Rapids: Baker, 1984), 453–54.

17. Gigi Graham Tchividjian and Ruth Bell Graham, *A Quiet Knowing* (Nashville: W Publishing Group, 2001), 5.

18. Charles Stanley, *Finding Peace* (Nashville: Thomas Nelson, 2003), 27.

19. Anderson and Miller, 52.

20. Reeni Fenholt, *Integrity of a Father* (Enumclaw, Wash.: WinePress Publishing, 2002), 67.

21. Gary and Barbara Rosberg, *The Five Love Needs of Men & Women* (Wheaton, Ill.: Tyndale, 2000), 15–16.

22. David S. Dockery, gen. ed., *Holman Bible Handbook* (Nashville: Holman Bible Publishers, 1992), 812.

23. McGee, 100.

24. H. Norman Wright, *Freedom from the Grip of Fear* (Grand Rapids: Fleming H. Revell, 2003), 75.

25. Normajean Hinders, *Seasons of a Woman's Life* (Nashville: Broadman and Holman, 1994), 177–78.

Week 6: A Time to Heal, A Time for Peace

1. Henry David Thoreau, *Walden and Other Writings* (New York: Bantam Books, 1989), 160.

2. Kevin Leman, *When Your Best Isn't Good Enough* (Grand Rapids: Baker/Fleming H. Revell, 1988), 23.

3. H. Norman Wright, *Making Peace with Your Past* (Grand Rapids: Baker Book House/Fleming H. Revell, 1985, 2004), 22.

4. H. Norman Wright, *The Key to Your Man's Heart* (Ventura, Calif.: Regal, 2004), 73.

5. H. Norman Wright, *Always Daddy's Girl* (Ventura, Calif.: Regal, 1989), 137–38.

6. Ibid., 160–61.

7. Denise George, *Cultivating a Forgiving Heart* (Grand Rapids: Zondervan, 2004), 36.

8. Charles Colson, *Answers to Your Kids' Questions* (Wheaton, Ill.: Tyndale, 2000), 17.

9. St. Augustine, quoted in C. S. Lewis, *The Four Loves* (New York: Phoenix Press, 1960), 204.

10. Lloyd John Ogilvie, *God's Best for My Life* (Eugene, Ore.: Harvest House, 1981), 1.

11. Diane Passno, *Feminism: Mystique or Mistake?* (Wheaton, Ill.: Tyndale, 2000), 170.

12. Harold H. Bloomfield with Leonard Felder, *Making Peace with Your Parents* (New York: Ballantine Books, 1983), 200.

13. Chap and Dee Clark, *Daughters and Dads* (Colorado Springs: NavPress, 1998), 160.

14. Robert S. McGee, *Search for Significance* (Nashville: LifeWay, 1992), 101.

About the Author

Denise George is an author, speaker, teacher, wife, and mother. She has written more than 20 books, and speaks frequently (nationally and internationally) at women's Bible Study meetings, retreats, and seminars; as well as seminaries, colleges, and churches. She co-teaches "The Writing Minister" (with Dr. Calvin Miller) at Beeson Divinity School. Denise is married to Dr. Timothy George, founding dean of Beeson Divinity School, Samford University, Birmingham, Alabama. Denise and Timothy have written books together, and have worked side-by-side in inner-city ministry (Boston, Mass.), at Southern Baptist Theological Seminary (Louisville, Ky.), at Ruschlikon Theological Seminary (Ruschlikon/Zurich, Switzerland), and now make their home in Birmingham, Alabama. They have two grown children: Alyce Elizabeth, Christian Timothy and his wife, Rebecca Pounds.

Secrets of Soul Gardening

Denise George

Four devotional Bible study guides designed to help women connect individually with God and with each other in a weekly group

This deeply personal Bible study series is designed to stimulate your personal growth and explore the questions of life one-on-one with God. Each of the four six- to eight-week studies delves into the metaphor of gardening, with God as the Gardener of our lives. The studies help women connect with God on an individual basis for daily nurture as well as in a supportive weekly group study with other women. Denise George provides meaningful interaction with Scripture while sharing personal illustrations from her own life, offering a deep and challenging growth experience.

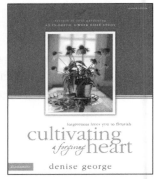

- *Tilling the Soul* is an eight-week study that inspires women to pray with faith and effectiveness, especially in the midst of difficult and painful experiences.
- *Cultivating a Forgiving Heart* is a six-week series leading women to understand why, how, and when to forgive, and, most important, helping them experience scriptural forgiveness and find anew freedom in Jesus Christ.
- *Weathering the Storms* is a six-week series that helps women develop a deep root system based in God's Word so that they can withstand the onslaught of any fear.

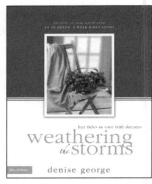

- *Planting Trust, Knowing Peace* is a six-week series helping women dispel distrust and learn to deepen their father-daughter relationship with their heavenly Father.

Tilling the Soul: Prayer Penetrates Your Pain	0-310-26743-9
Cultivating a Forgiving Heart: Forgiveness Frees You to Flourish	0-310-26744-7
Weathering the Storms: Fear Fades as Your Faith Deepens	0-310-25118-4
Planting Trust, Knowing Peace: Trust Grows as You Embrace the Father's Love	0-310-25119-2

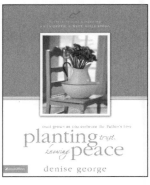

We want to hear from you. Please send your comments about this book to us in care of zreview@zondervan.com. Thank you.

GRAND RAPIDS, MICHIGAN 49530 USA

WWW.ZONDERVAN.COM

All Pathway to Purpose™ books work together to enhance a woman's journey as she searches for her God-given purpose. Each book provides its own unique benefit that enriches her walk down the pathway.

Pathway to Purpose™ for Women is a stand-alone book that takes the five universal purposes from *The Purpose-Driven® Life* and helps women drill down to their own unique life purposes. This book is also available as an Abridged Audio CD.

Conversations on Purpose for Women is a companion book to *Pathway to Purpose for Women*, specifically designed for those women who want to find another woman who can serve as their Purpose Partner to help them down the path toward purpose.

Praying for Purpose for Women is a 60-day prayer experience that can change a woman's life forever. Sixty influential Christian women share how *their* lives have changed.

Pathway to Purpose™ for Women Personal Journal allows women to reflect during their quiet time on how the principles they discover can and will affect their lives.

Pathway to Purpose™ for Women	0-310-25649-6
(In Spanish) *Camino hacia el propósito para mujeres*	08297-4506-8
Pathway to Purpose™ for Women Abridged Audio CD	0-310-26505-3
Conversations on Purpose for Women	0-310-25650-X
(In Spanish) *Conversaciones con propósito para mujeres*	08297-4508-4
Praying for Purpose for Women	0-310-25652-6
(In Spanish) *Oración con propósito para mujeres*	08297-4507-6
Pathway to Purpose™ for Women Personal Journal	0-310-81174-0

Spanish products available May, 2005.

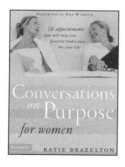 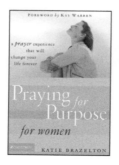